ESG — Can't believe it! I love you so. EP

Lessons from the Field

Unlocking Economic Potential With an Environmental Key

Edith M. Pepper

Northeast
Midwest
Institute

ISBN: 1-882061-64-0

Although the research described in this article has been funded wholly or in part by the United States Environmental Protection Agency, under assistance agreement CR824570-01-0 to the Northeast-Midwest Institute, it has not been subjected to the Agency's peer and administrative review and therefore may not necessarily reflect the views of the Agency and no official endorsement should be inferred.

Northeast-Midwest Institute

The Northeast-Midwest Institute is a nonprofit and public education organization that seeks to enhance the region's economic vitality and environmental quality. It conducts research, develops public policies, provides technical assistance, sponsors regional conferences, and distributes publications.

The Institute is unique among Washington policy centers because of its close working relationship with the Northeast-Midwest Congressional and Senate Coalitions. Founded in 1976, the Congressional Coalition, co-chaired by Reps. Bob Franks (R-NJ) and Marty Meehan (D-MA), is a bipartisan group of 114 representatives who recognize the common problems facing their states. The Northeast-Midwest Senate Coalition, formed in 1978 and now co-chaired by Sens. James Jeffords (R-VT) and Daniel Patrick Moynihan (D-NY), has 36 members.

Northeast-Midwest Institute
218 D Street, S.E.
Washington, D.C. 20003
(202) 544-5200
(202) 544-0043 (fax)
http://www.nemw.org

Table of Contents

CHAPTER 1
Introduction

Introduction

Across the nation, cities and small towns are grappling with the challenge of abandoned or under-utilized, often contaminated, industrial properties — also known as "brownfields." Brownfield reuse has captured public attention because it offers the unique opportunity to solve multiple problems concurrently, a particularly attractive prospect for government officials.

With minimal public investment, brownfield projects may provide environmental cleanup, reduce neighborhood blight, generate tax revenues, and create jobs — all of which helps to stabilize and enrich a community. These redevelopments usually make use of existing infrastructure, such as highways and utilities, thus maximizing the benefit of previously spent public dollars. In addition, brownfield reuse offsets development that might have occurred on rural or suburban properties, known as "greenfields," thus helping to limit urban sprawl — an increasingly high priority for many Americans.

Despite these opportunities, many challenges frustrate brownfield reuse. The overarching deterrent, most stakeholders conclude, is "uncertainty." Older, industrial properties introduce a series of unknowns having to do with environmental conditions, costs, time frames, and long-term liability. By contrast, locating projects on greenfields is commonly thought to be a cheaper, more predictable alternative.

By 1996, local, state, and federal officials had championed a series of innovative policies aimed at encouraging the reuse of contaminated sites, and an increasing number of brownfield projects were being launched. The Northeast-Midwest Institute felt that it was critical to understand the connection between these trends — to gauge which policies are most effectively encouraging redevelopment "on the ground." With support from the U.S. Environmental Protection Agency (EPA), the Institute assumed a case study approach, one that involved selecting 20 brownfield projects, researching site histories, and interviewing more than 60 participants. The goal was to understand how certain projects overcame the barriers typically associated with brownfield reuse and then to derive a series of "lessons learned" from the field — including innovative financing strategies, creative public-private partnerships, and state voluntary cleanup programs — that could be shared with other locales facing similar challenges.

Lessons from the Field complements several Northeast-Midwest Institute books that analyze brownfield policy issues, particularly *Coming Clean For Economic Development: A Resource Book on Environmental Cleanup and Economic Development Opportunities (September 1996, 178 pages)*, which contains an in-depth discussion of the challenges associated with brownfield reuse, several case studies, and an overview of state initiatives.

Northeast-Midwest Institute staff, in developing *Lessons from the Field*, have attempted to reflect the diversity of brownfield sites nationwide by choosing case studies from many different settings. Nine of the projects were located in large metropolitan areas (over 250,000 population); seven in medium cities (between 50,000 and 250,000) and four in small communities (under 50,000). The Institute also chose different sized projects. Some were quite large — such as the $200-million Medical City initiative in Worcester, Massachusetts, that involved cleaning up and reusing 24 acres of blighted downtown property, and which is expected to create 3,000 new jobs and have a total direct economic impact of $875 million within its first ten years of operation. Other projects were smaller in scale, although no less important for their communities. For example, redevelopment of the Carol Cable plant in Warren, Rhode Island, brought 75 existing jobs to the area and created 50 new ones — good news for this town of 11,000.

The remainder of this chapter contains brief synopses of the 20 brownfield projects profiled, divided by region.

Property Transactions Among Case Studies

The 20 case studies examined in this book represent three main types of property transactions: purchaser driven, public-sector driven, and private-sector driven. For most of the projects, local government played a critical role.

Purchaser Driven: Redevelopment by Purchaser with Strong State and Local Assistance

(city-coordinated transfer of privately-owned land)

- Medical City, Worcester, Massachusetts
- Southwest Harbor Project, Seattle, Washington
- Carol Cable, Warren, Rhode Island
- Acetex Corp., Detroit, Michigan
- Northeast Retail Project, Minneapolis, Minnesota
- American Axle & Manufacturing (the project's parkway segment), Buffalo, New York

(city-coordinated transfer of city-owned land)

- Louisville Dryer Company, Louisville, Kentucky
- Scott Peterson Meats, Chicago, Illinois
- Madison Equipment, Chicago, Illinois
- Holden-Leonard Mill, Bennington, Vermont

Public-Sector Driven: Redevelopment by Local or State Government on Privately-Owned Brownfields

- Bryant Electric, Bridgeport, Connecticut
- Lawrence Gateway Project, Lawrence, Massachusetts
- Circle F Factory, Trenton, New Jersey
- Crosby Lake Business Park, St. Paul, Minnesota
- Oregon Mill Site Conversion Project, Seven Oregon Counties

Private-Sector Driven: Redevelopment by Private Entity on Privately-Owned Brownfield

(city played key role)

- Federal Courthouse/Southern Pacific Rail Yard, Sacramento, California
- BASF South Works, Wyandotte, Michigan

(city played minor role)

- Roundhouse Property, Wilmington, Delaware
- Ernst Steel Site, Cheektowaga, New York
- Ross's Landing and Aquarium, Chattanooga, Tennessee
- American Axle Plant (the project's paint facility segment), Buffalo, New York

End Uses for Case Study Sites

Sites	Names of Sites	Starting Use of Property	End Use of Property
8	Acetex Corp., Detroit, Michigan Madison Equipment, Chicago, IL Louisville Dryer Co., Louisville, KY Scott Peterson Meats, Chicago, IL Roundhouse Property, Wilmington, DE American Axle Plant, Buffalo, NY Southwest Harbor, Seattle, WA Carol Cable, Warren, RI	Industrial	Industrial (Note: three of these projects — Madison Equipment, Louisville Dryer Co., and Acetex — were expansions made by neighboring businesses.)
4	Oregon Mill Sites, 7 Oregon Counties Crosby Lake Business Park, St. Paul, MN Bryant Electric, Bridgeport, CT Holden-Leonard Mill, Bennington, VT	Industrial	Light Industry, Offices, Business Park
3	Ernst Steel, Cheektowaga, NY Northeast Retail Center, Minneapolis, MN Ross's Landing and Aquarium, Chattanooga, TN	Industrial	Commercial, Shopping Center
2	Lawrence Gateway Project, Lawrence, MA BASF South Works, Wyandotte, MI	Industrial	Recreational, Transportation
1	Circle F Project, Trenton, NJ	Industrial	Half Residential, Half Industrial
1	Federal Courthouse / Southern Pacific Railyard, Sacramento, CA	Industrial	Mixed Use: Commercial, Residential, Industrial
1	Medical City, Worcester, MA	Industrial	Hospital
Total 20			

Midwest

BASF South Works, Wyandotte, Michigan

This project involved transforming a defunct, 84-acre chemical manufacturing plant along the Detroit River into a public recreation area and a nine-hole golf course. Through a combination of pubic and private funding (the city utilized tax increment financing, state grants, and bonds), the city was able to revitalize the waterfront and the once-blighted neighborhood around BASF's plant. This redevelopment has precipitated a domino effect of economic growth throughout downtown Wyandotte. BASF's project highlights the importance of a strong public/private partnership, as well as illustrates how a large company can use brownfield cleanup to bolster its corporate image.

Acetex Corporation, Detroit, Michigan

In the early 1990s, Acetex Corporation, a Detroit-based textile manufacturing enterprise, sought to expand its operations by acquiring an adjacent property, H&H Wheel Service, Inc. Acetex planned to build a new $5-million distribution facility on the two-acre site, creating over 100 new jobs in the process. But H&H Wheel was reluctant to sell its property unless the firm could be cleared of all liability (environmental conditions at the site were not yet known) and absolved of any costs associated with cleanup. The deal was finalized after a year of negotiating, during which the Detroit REUS Team, an inter-agency brownfield task force, played a pivotal role. In 1995, EPA awarded the City of Detroit a $200,000 Brownfields Pilot Site grant in support of the REUS Team's ongoing activities.

Scott Peterson Meats, Chicago, Illinois

In 1993, Scott Peterson Meats approached the City of Chicago with a proposition. The company was interested in acquiring an adjacent, abandoned property on which it would provide secure parking for its employees. If the city could arrange the deal, Scott Peterson Meats promised to expand its existing operations and hire new employees, thus providing a stable business presence in an increasingly blighted neighborhood. By May 1995, only 13 months after the project began, the city had remediated the site and prepared to turn it over to Scott Peterson Meats. This project illustrates how carefully targeted public spending can leverage significant private investment. The city spent only $370,000 to clean and grade this site; Scott Peterson Meats, in turn, invested $5.2 million in a new smokehouse and hired 100 new local employees. This case study also points to the effectiveness of Chicago's Brownfields Program, an innovative policy-development initiative.

Madison Equipment, Chicago, Illinois

Madison Equipment, a 70-employee firm in Chicago's East Garfield Park neighborhood, sought to acquire an abandoned building in the early 1990s to accommodate its business expansion needs. The city agreed to complete a site investigation (which revealed significantly less contamination than officials had feared) and to transfer the property to Madison for $1 dollar. In return, Madison pledged to rehabilitate the building and hire at least 6-8 workers from the federal Empowerment Zone in which it's located. Expending only $3,000 in public funds, the city was able to eliminate a community eyesore, assist a strong neighborhood business in its expansion efforts, and create new jobs.

Crosby Lake Business Park (Texaco Tank Farm),
St. Paul, Minnesota

The St. Paul Port Authority had long sought to redevelop Texaco's 40-acre tank farm, located in a commercial/industrial corridor in southwest St. Paul. After scaling back its presence in the region, Texaco removed several above-ground tanks in the 1980s. In spring 1993, the port authority, Texaco, and the Minnesota Pollution Control Agency formally began to discuss the site's future use. During negotiations, Texaco agreed to remediate the site and then sell it to the port authority for roughly fair market value. The port would grade the site and provide infrastructure improvements, creating a new business park in the process. The port authority spent $6.2 million to purchase and improve the site, costs that are slated to be recovered within ten years. Officials estimate that the new complex will create 350 jobs and generate $640,000 in new annual property taxes. Ten of the 40 acres were deeded to the St. Paul Parks and Recreational Department as part of the Mississippi River Open Space Area. Participants emphasize that the success of this project hinged on a strong public/private partnership.

Northeast Retail Project (Johnson Street Quarry),
Minneapolis, Minnesota

By the 1990s, the once-active Johnson Street Quarry had become a blighted, under-utilized property that contributed to the economic decline of northeast Minneapolis. In 1993, the Ryan Company, a local developer, approached the city with a plan. If the Minneapolis Community Development Agency (MCDA) acquired various quarry parcels and conducted necessary reme-diation, Ryan would purchase the site for twice its market value (which, even then, would be significantly less than the public costs to prepare the site) and build a 420,000-square foot discount shopping mall. As of late 1996, all properties had been acquired and remediation had begun. Project costs are expected to total nearly $60 million, divided between public and private sources. Despite high expenditures, the MCDA views the deal as public funds well spent. Benefits include extensive environmental cleanup, blight elimination, creation of 1,700 full- and part-time jobs, tax-base enhancements (both property and sales), and stabilization of a neighborhood that had been declining. The city will recoup its costs within 15 years through property taxes and revenues generated from the tax increment finance district. This project involved extensive community involvement, as well as strong public/private cooperation.

Northeast

Holden-Leonard Mill, Bennington, Vermont

In 1986, backed by state and federal loans, the Southern Vermont Development Council bought the defunct Holden-Leonard Mill and planned a series of renovations. Three years later, however, the project stalled when U.S. EPA alleged the presence of hazardous contamination on site. Since 1989, the mill has remained in limbo while EPA has debated listing the site on the National Priorities List (NPL), a register of the country's most serious hazardous waste sites. Mase Securities International (MSI), currently a tenant in the Holden-Leonard Mill, is eager to purchase the site but will not proceed until all environmental and liability issues have been resolved. In April, 1996, EPA Region 1 issued a "comfort letter" to the mill's new owner, the Vermont Economic Development Authority, indicating that no further steps would be taken to list the site on the NPL, thus removing a crucial barrier to the site's redevelopment. At the same time, MSI has been able to benefit from Vermont's new voluntary cleanup law, which provides liability relief for third parties upon completion of an approved cleanup plan. To date, MSI has created over 200 new jobs in Bennington and has made significant renovations to the historic building.

Fallon/St. Vincent Medical City, Worcester, Massachusetts

In 1992, two of the largest health care providers in Worcester merged with the hope of building a $200-million integrated health facility in an urban setting. Eager to attract the hospital, city officials immediately created an institution to oversee the endeavor — the Worcester Redevelopment Authority — and began targeting properties within a 24-acre blighted area for acquisition. By 1996, all structures had been demolished and the graded property was conveyed to the purchaser for $6.4 million with a Covenant-Not-to-Sue. Total public expenditures on the project were $42 million, split between the state and the city. City officials expect to see a huge return on their investment. Once operational, the facility will provide nearly 3,000 new jobs and will generate $875 million in total direct economic impacts within the first ten years ($1.9 billion in indirect economic impacts). This case study illustrates how strong public/private cooperation can save time and produce immense cost-savings. It also demonstrates the importance of establishing an effective institutional framework — in this case, the Worcester Redevelopment Authority — to oversee brownfield redevelopment activities.

Lawrence Gateway Project (Oxford Paper Site),
Lawrence, Massachusetts

Like many industrial cities across the country, Lawrence, Massachusetts, has in recent years witnessed a steady decline in manufacturing. Many residents believe that the key to future growth lies in either revitalizing the city's once-thriving mills or at least reusing the valuable waterfront property on which they stand. One of Lawrence's most prominent brownfields is the mammoth Oxford Paper plant, located at the entrance or "gateway" to the city's historical district. In 1994, officials launched an initiative to redevelop the Oxford site that involved "piggy-backing" the project onto a nearby highway project, thus enabling the city to draw on Massachusetts Highway Department funds. Plans call for demolition of existing Oxford buildings, construction of road interchanges, and creation of a public park. This project has been successful on many fronts. Officials were able to streamline permitting and oversight activities by creating two interagency task forces. The project was propelled forward by a strong public/private partnership between the city and GenCorp, Oxford's neighbor. In addition, city officials made public participation a priority from the outset. In its first two years, the Lawrence Gateway Project has leveraged over $160 million in public and private investment for Lawrence's historic district.

Carol Cable Site, Warren, Rhode Island

This project involved redevelopment of a 240,000-square-foot cable manufacturing factory in a small town of population 11,000. The facility closed down in 1990 and was remediated under state supervision, but residual contaminants remained on-site (the company was unable to achieve the state's stringent water quality standards). In fall 1995, Display World, Inc. expressed an interest in purchasing the site, but not until the state resolved all environmental issues and provided liability releases. State officials made it a priority to meet Display World's needs in a timely fashion. Strong inter-agency coordination helped decrease costs and reduce time-frames associated with the project. Most importantly, Rhode Island's 1995 brownfield law made the transaction possible by providing the purchaser with necessary liability sign-off. Also critical was the recent adoption of state cleanup standards that allow for the use of institutional/engineering controls to satisfy remedial requirements. Display World purchased the property for $175,000 and then proceeded to invest $500,000 in the facility. The company brought 75 existing jobs to the area and plans to create 50 new ones.

Bryant Electric Plant, Bridgeport, Connecticut

Westinghouse's Bryant Electric plant shut down in 1988 after operating for 90 years in Bridgeport's West End. The closing of the 500,000-square-foot facility exacerbated the neighborhood's already bleak economic situation. In the early 1990s, the city began working with Westinghouse and area businesses to discuss plans for revitalizing the entire West End, using redevelopment at the Bryant Electric site as a catalyst. A plan emerged whereby the city agreed to acquire seven acres of property around Bryant Electric, essentially forming a large business park. An important step in this process was the 1994 formation of the West End Community Development Corporation (CDC), a non-profit development group. In just two years, the CDC has succeeded in organizing many different voices within the West End, developing a strong vision for growth, and providing the institutional framework necessary to implement community goals. Westinghouse has spent over $1 million to date on remediation at its site, while the city and the CDC (backed by state funds) have invested over $14 million in Bryant Electric and the West End, as a whole. According to city officials, the targeted developer plans to create 300-400 new jobs and invest $20-$50 million in the West End.

Circle F Factory, Trenton, New Jersey

The 1990 closing of the Circle F factory left a gaping hole in Trenton's East Ward. For over 100 years, the facility had been the heart of this neighborhood; now the area was becoming increasingly mired in economic decline. Working with the property owner, the city devised a solution that involved dividing the Circle F factory in half and developing the parcels separately (one would contain light industry; the other would be transformed into seniors' housing). For the residential portion of the project, the city selected Lutheran

Social Ministries (LSM), an experienced non-profit developer. In June 1995, LSM applied for and received federal Low-Income Housing Tax Credits — an innovative financing mechanism that can assist brownfield projects. Additional remediation took place in fall 1995 and construction of 75 new senior housing units began at the end of that year. Residents are slated to move in by winter 1997.

American Axle Plant and Northeast Buffalo Parkway, Buffalo, New York

In February 1994, American Axle & Manufacturing bought a struggling automotive plant in Buffalo, with the hope of investing nearly $100 million at the site. Company officials pledged to retain 1,000 jobs and add 600 more — good news for Northeast Buffalo, which had weathered a major GM-plant closing four years earlier. Without improved truck access to the American Axle site, however, the company could not follow through with its plans to increase operations and bring on new employees. City officials recognized that this was not only a problem for American Axle; poor infrastructure had caused numerous area industries to relocate to the suburbs. Officials decided to transform into a highway an old, rarely used stretch of Conrail tracks traversing Northeast Buffalo (the road would be called the Northeast Buffalo Parkway). American Axle's $100-million investment helped leverage $6.5 million in public funds for the deal. With construction of the highway slated to begin in 1997, benefits to the surrounding neighborhood already can be seen. The defunct GM plant now has been transformed into a light industrial park that could employ 200 people in the near future. Most importantly, however, city officials believe that the presence of these viable industries and improved highway access will trigger a revival of the Northeast Buffalo neighborhood.

Ernst Steel Site, Cheektowaga, New York

Before closing down in 1980, the Ernst Steel site had operated for over 30 years in Cheektowaga, New York, a town located just outside the Buffalo city line. By 1990, the Buffalo suburbs had expanded outward, completely surrounding Ernst Steel, but the site remained idle and undeveloped due to concerns over environmental contamination. In 1994, the Benderson Development Company bought the property out of bankruptcy court with the intention of building a discount shopping center. The company struck a deal with Erie County officials: If the county provided tax breaks on another project Benderson was initiating (construction of a nearby hotel), the developer would agree to completely remediate the Ernst Steel site, which had become a glaring eyesore in this heavily commercialized area. Benderson also wagered that the project's long-term economic benefits would far outweigh the short-term cleanup costs. To defray remediation expenses, the company successfully employed a new technology, on-site soil-washing. Redevelopment of the Ernst Steel site has resulted in many positive impacts, including elimination of blight, creation of 150 full- and part-time jobs, and tax base enhancement (sales taxes will be $1 million per year; property taxes between $300,000 and $500,000 per year).

The Roundhouse Property (Harlan & Hollingsworth Shipyard), Wilmington, Delaware

The roundhouse is an old railroad turnstile located in Wilmington's former Harlan & Hollingsworth Shipyard. Closed in the 1950s, various shipyard buildings have been dispersed over the years. Many of the structures now are abandoned or under-utilized, and environmental contamination is widespread. The 1.6-acre roundhouse property is no exception. When the current owner decided to sell the property, the interested buyer stipulated that environmental issues needed to be resolved up front. Both parties decided to enter Delaware's voluntary cleanup program in order to conduct remediation, obtain liability sign-off, and apply for state financial assistance. The Delaware Department of Natural Resources and Environmental Control pursued an innovative funding source for the project: federal Superfund dollars funneled through the state. The buyer plans to construct a public storage facility which will create new jobs and provide a stable business presence in the neighborhood. This case study illustrates how brownfield activities can dovetail successfully with a city's broader redevelopment visions.

West

Oregon Mill Site Conversion Project,
Seven rural areas in Oregon

During the 1980s and 1990s, over 120 timber mills shut down in the Pacific Northwest, displacing 55,000 workers and devastating many timber-dependent communities. For years these mill sites sat idle and undeveloped while chemical hazards posed environmental and public health concerns. In 1994, a group of public agencies and private-sector groups joined forces in an effort to redevelop seven rural mill sites. The initiative, known as the Oregon Mill Site Conversion Project, received financial backing from both U.S. EPA, under its Brownfields Pilot Site Program, and the Economic Development Administration. During its first two years, the project has focused on organizing community participation and assessing the environmental conditions at each site. Thus far, two sites already have changed hands and should be cleaned up and redeveloped by fall 1997.

Southwest Harbor Project, Seattle, Washington

In 1993, an Oakland-based steamship company, American President Lines, Ltd. (APL), asked the Port of Seattle to compete with other west coast ports to develop a combined marine cargo and intermodal terminal yard that would be large enough to handle APL's increasing Pacific Rim trade. To meet APL's needs, the terminal had to be fully operational by 1997 — only four years away. Seattle port officials were anxious to keep APL's existing 1,500 jobs and to secure 1,500 additional jobs through the terminal expansion. The project also would provide a catalyst for the remediation of other properties in the Duwamish corridor, a heavily industrialized area with known contamination problems. The port identified 145 acres around APL's existing terminal and initiated negotiations with current property owners (hurdles included assessing environmental conditions, determining necessary remediation, and accurately gauging property values). The project involved unprecedented coordination between local, state, and federal agencies. It also required extensive public participation. As of summer 1996, all buildings had been demolished and most remediation was complete on APL's new terminal property.

Federal Courthouse (Southern Pacific Rail Yard),
Sacramento, California

The 2.6-acre federal courthouse project is located on Southern Pacific's 244-acre railyard facility in Sacramento. The $142 million, 380,000-square-foot courthouse facility, which will contain offices, parking, and many other services, is slated to produce more than 1,000 construction jobs and 200 permanent jobs. It is the single largest construction project in the City of Sacramento's history. A major challenge associated with this project was the presence of deed restrictions, which required direct state oversight of all excavation activities — a daunting mandate given the limited resources of the state environmental agency. Through extensive public/private cooperation, an innovative third-party oversight entity was established, known as the Environmental Oversight Authority. Creation of this institutional entity allowed redevelopment to proceed where it otherwise might have been deemed logistically and economically impossible. In July 1995, EPA awarded the city a $200,000 Brownfields Pilot Site grant to support the Environmental Oversight Authority and other aspects of the railyard redevelopment.

South

Ross's Landing and the Tennessee Aquarium,
Chattanooga, Tennessee

Chattanooga, once considered a leading industrial powerhouse, paid a high price for its economic prosperity. By the late 1960s, it was named one of the most polluted cities in America. In the decades since, however, Chattanooga has made a swift comeback. A key step in this process has been the cleanup and reuse of former industrial properties. In the 1980s, a public/private non-profit development company — RiverValley Partners — was formed to manage the city's redevelopment plans. The company initially focused its efforts on a stretch of old industrial property along the Tennessee River and raised nearly $17 million in private funds to support acquisition, environmental assessments, and construction of a new aquarium and public plaza. According to company officials, the Tennessee Aquarium has been a catalyst for more than $150 million in public and private investment throughout Chattanooga.

Louisville Dryer Company (Ni-Chro Plating, Inc.),
Louisville, Kentucky

The Ni-Chro Plating facility in Louisville's West End had been abandoned for several years when state officials discovered that the site presented an immediate threat to public and environmental health. The U.S. EPA conducted an emergency removal of contaminants and, because the prior owner was bankrupt, placed a lien on the property for $168,000. Seven years later, in 1994, the Louisville Dryer Company expressed an interest in purchasing the Ni-Chro Plating property in order to accommodate its business expansion — a move that would create new jobs and add to the local tax base, both of which the city was eager to support. In 1995, when U.S. EPA awarded Louisville a $200,000 Brownfields Pilot grant, the city decided to dedicate this money to the Ni-Chro Plating project, which essentially would serve as a "demonstration site" for implementation of city-wide brownfield policies. As of late 1996, the city and the Louisville Dryer Company were negotiating a final sale price for the property. This project is poised to become a brownfield success story — neighborhood blight is being eliminated at the same time that 40-50 new jobs are being created.

This chapter has provided an overview of the 20 brownfield projects profiled in this book. Chapter 2 includes a discussion of key conclusions or "lessons learned" through the case study analysis. Chapter 3 presents the case studies, themselves.

CHAPTER 2
Lessons Learned

Lessons Learned

Encouraging the cleanup and redevelopment of brownfields requires a comprehensive package of solutions — some direct, some indirect — that become relevant at different points in the process. For example, many case study participants note that financial incentives and liability relief are critical in terms of persuading individuals to undertake projects in the first place. However, other factors — such as inter-agency coordination and project leadership at the local level — assume greater importance once a project is underway by helping to slash time frames and save costs.

Examination of a wide range of sites, as well as over 60 interviews with project participants, revealed some common components or "lessons learned," which are divided into five groupings: a) players and institutional capacity; b) community involvement; c) regulatory and legal issues; d) costs and financing; d) risk management and cleanup; and e) broader policy conclusions. Following are the key factors that facilitated brownfield cleanup and reuse.

Players and Institutional Capacity

Presence of a Proactive Local Government Entity or Redevelopment Authority

Among these case studies, one of the most critical ingredients for success was the presence of a strong local government entity. For half the projects examined, the city acted as a "brownfield broker," essentially helping interested buyers acquire contaminated and/or abandoned properties. For several other projects, the city played a key role in helping a company clean up and redevelop its contaminated site, as well as locating potential buyers or end-users. Local officials also were invaluable in terms of facilitating community involvement and helping parties navigate difficult regulatory requirements.

In addition to playing a key logistical role, cities often provided financing to make a brownfield project economically viable. In Bridgeport, Connecticut, Westinghouse has spent over $1 million to clean up its Bryant Electric facility, and the city contributed $700,000 towards demolition and site preparation to make way for a new end-user. Without the city's involvement, the site might only have been remediated and not actually redeveloped.

In Louisville, Kentucky, the city has been working with an expanding business to acquire an abandoned, contaminated property. This project has been complicated by many factors, including environmental contamination at the site and uncertain remediation requirements. The city oversaw relations between the Kentucky Department of Environmental Protection, the Landbank Authority, and the prospective purchaser, Louisville Dryer Company. In addition, the city dedicated funds to this project (for personnel and site assessment) from grant money provided under the U.S. Environmental Protection Agency's (EPA) Brownfields Pilot Site Program. Because of the city's involvement, Louisville Dryer Co. has been able to remain involved in a real estate transaction that it might otherwise have abandoned long ago.

Appropriate Institutional Capacity at the Local Level — Consolidating Brownfield Project Management Teams Under One Roof

While cities clearly play an essential role in brownfield redevelopment, often they are not set up to effectively manage such projects. The problem is that brownfield initiatives require involvement by personnel from a range of departments (e.g., planning, law, economic development, and environmental protection), which can create administrative snafus. In addition, efforts can be complicated by the fact that these departments often have conflicting missions and mandates. All project participants interviewed for this book agree that establishing a *single* entity for oversight of brownfield initiatives is key. The Worcester Redevelopment Authority (WRA) in Worcester, Massachusetts, is an example of such an entity. The WRA acquires properties, coordinates remediation, and facilitates site redevelopment work. Similarly, the Port of Seattle assembled under one lead manager a group of staff members who were dedicated to the Southwest Harbor redevelopment project. This team, which worked out of one office location, included members of the port's marine facilities as well as staff from legal, engineering, environmental, and finance offices.

Strong Public-Private Partnerships

Among the 20 case studies, public/private partnerships — usually between private parties, the city, and the state — were essential. In particular, those locales that forged alliances between business interests and public-sector objectives have seen significant results. In Wyandotte, Michigan, BASF, the City of Wyandotte, and the Michigan Department of Environmental Quality teamed up to redevelop BASF's South Works into a public recreation area. In St. Paul, Minnesota, the St. Paul Port Authority and the Minneapolis Pollution Control Agency worked with Texaco to transform an old petroleum tank farm into a new light industrial business park.

In several instances, partnerships between project participants and politicians also proved to be important, especially in terms of obtaining much-needed public funding. The Lawrence Gateway Project, for example, benefitted from strong involvement by Congressman Marty Meehan (D-MA). Rep. Meehan helped secure a $25,000 grant from the Massachusetts Land Bank as well as $500,000 in roadway enhancement funds for the project through the Intermodal Surface Transportation Efficiency Act.

Project Leadership — Individuals Make A Difference

Many of these projects have been successful because of certain key individuals who possess strong leadership, persistence, and creativity. For example, in Sacramento, California, the federal courthouse development has been spearheaded by the city's Wendy Saunders. When Saunders took maternity leave over the summer of 1996, many participants indicated that the project was "virtually on hold" until she returned. The same has been true of Kevin Geaney with the Lawrence Gateway Project in Lawrence, Massachusetts. For years, redevelopment of the city's Oxford Paper site was at a standstill; when Lawrence hired Geaney, however, the process finally began to move forward. Several people interviewed indicate that he was the catalyst for launching the Lawrence Gateway Project.

Coordination Between Local, State, and Federal Government Entities

Many brownfield projects are burdened by high assessment and remediation costs and by long, drawn-out time frames — a situation that is only exacerbated when multiple government agencies (i.e., local, state, and federal) are involved. For many of the projects examined, streamlining inter-agency coordination was critical in terms of resolving overlaps in administrative jurisdictions and oversight. Lawrence, Massachusetts, tackled this problem by establishing two inter-agency task forces — teams comprised of local, state, and federal representatives — that ironed out key issues, facilitated decision making, and coordinated the multiple regulatory issues connected with the project. In Sacramento, California, redevelopment of Southern Pacific's rail yard was made possible by an innovative Memorandum of Understanding (MOU) between the city, the state, and Southern Pacific. The MOU articulated roles and responsibilities for each party and established a third-party oversight entity, the Environmental Oversight Authority, which was tasked with overseeing all site assessment and cleanup in lieu of the state environmental agency.

Community Involvement

Strong Community Participation

In almost every case study analyzed, carefully orchestrated public outreach and involvement plans were implemented from the outset. Without this critical community buy-in, many project participants note, their efforts easily could have fallen apart. In Minneapolis, community participation was central to the redevelopment of the Johnson Street Quarry into a discount shopping center. The Minneapolis Community Development Agency assembled a neighborhood task force, which met monthly in a televised public forum to discuss project plans. In a written report, the group expressed numerous concerns about traffic, noise, and public safety and called on the city to implement a series of traffic control measures and infrastructure improvements before it would support the initiative. The city and developers unanimously agreed to meet the task force's demands, and the project moved forward with strong public support.

Capitalizing on a Community's Vision

Most case study participants agree that brownfield initiatives should dovetail with a community's "vision" for growth. For example, where brownfield redevelopment is part of a concerted downtown revitalization program, it stands a better chance of securing public and private investment, as well as gaining political and community support. In Chattanooga, Tennessee, cleanup and reuse of riverfront property dovetailed with the city's broader Vision 2000 initiative that sought to revitalize neighborhoods, remediate the environment, and attract new businesses throughout the city.

Appropriate Job Training

Many communities are eager to ensure that brownfield redevelopment and the presence of new business translate into job opportunities for area residents. Job training often is necessary to ensure that residents acquire the appropriate skills. In St. Paul, Minnesota, the St. Paul Port Authority launched an innovative job training program, the Employment Connection, which helps link brownfield redevelopment with neighborhood wealth creation. The port determines the specific employment needs of local businesses, connects with various neighborhood groups, and creates a customized training package for companies. Businesses pay 10-15 percent of the costs for the training package; the balance is provided by the state and private corporations/foundations. This program will help ensure that area residents are properly trained for job openings at the Crosby Lake Business Park.

Regulatory and Legal Issues

State Voluntary Cleanup Programs — Availability of Liability Relief

As of December 1996, 37 states had established programs encouraging voluntary cleanup of contaminated sites. These state initiatives — many of which offer financial incentives, liability relief, and simplified cleanup standards — have significantly encouraged brownfield cleanup and reuse. For example, the contaminated Holden-Leonard Mill in Bennington, Vermont, was in a holding pattern for years, despite the fact that a party was interested in buying the site. With the enactment of Vermont's 1994 Contaminated Properties Program, however, site assessment and cleanup are now proceeding. One key reason is that both the seller and prospective purchaser now can obtain some liability closure once a state-approved cleanup plan has been completed.

Clarity Between the State and U.S. EPA in terms of Liability Relief

Although many states are offering some form of liability relief, participants interviewed still consider "fear of EPA involvement" a barrier to redevelopment, particularly in terms of securing financial backing. The agency has responded by stating publicly its intention not to interfere at sites that are participating in state voluntary cleanup programs. Some regional EPA offices have put this commitment in writing by including "comfort language" in their Superfund Memoranda of Agreement with states. These moves to bless state voluntary cleanup programs have been greeted favorably by brownfield practitioners.

Costs and Financing

Property Location and Market Conditions

The old real estate adage, "location, location, location," applies to brownfields as it would to any other property. If a brownfield is situated in a desirable location — near a bustling downtown, along a scenic waterfront, or by a busy highway interchange — redevelopment is more likely to occur than not, in spite of potential environmental contamination. In other words, the economics of the project may make sense even when costs for cleanup are factored into the equation. For example, Southern Pacific decided to remediate its Sacramento railyard facility as well as to pursue redevelopment because the company saw potentially huge profits (due to the site's prominent downtown location). Similarly, in Chattanooga, Tennessee, RiverValley Partners decided to purchase and redevelop old industrial property along the Tennessee River, wagering that any contamination discovered would be offset by huge returns on the investment.

However, if a brownfield is situated in an economically depressed area — on the outskirts of town or in a blighted neighborhood — redevelopment is a more difficult proposition. In these cases, the role of the public sector to encourage brownfield reuse becomes critical. The threat of environmental contamination is a major deterrent, but there may be other concerns: neighborhood safety for employees, blighted conditions surrounding the site, access to skilled labor, or the potential for property devaluation. In these cases, the city or the state may offer financial incentives to companies willing to locate in economically disadvantaged areas. Alternatively, the city may assist in redeveloping a portion of a neighborhood — as was the case in Bridgeport's West End, surrounding the Bryant Electric facility — in order to trigger a domino effect of revitalization.

Possibility of "Piggy-Backing" onto Public Works Projects

Brownfield projects may be coordinated with public works initiatives — including transportation projects, historic preservation efforts, and green corridor planning — in order to access innovative funding sources. In Lawrence, Massachusetts, for example, cleanup and redevelopment of the old Oxford Paper plant seemed financially infeasible until city personnel thought to "piggy-back" the project with a nearby highway expansion, allowing Lawrence to draw on much-needed state highway funds for demolition and remediation.

Benefit of Being a Large Development Company

Brownfield projects present less of a financial risk to large development companies, which can essentially distribute risk among different projects. These firms also may be able to finance initiatives themselves, without the involvement of banks, enabling them to take on projects of greater risk. In recent years, developers have become increasingly interested in contaminated sites. According to *Crain's New York Business* from November 1996, "Once seen only as a blight... [brownfields] are now becoming an opportunity for a number of savvy real estate developers." This sentiment is echoed by an attorney for Benderson Development Company (developer of the Ernst Steel site in Cheektowaga, New York), who notes, "Benderson views brownfields as the last frontier on which to make money."

Availability of Public-Sector Financing

Private parties frequently are not able or willing to act on their own to ensure that a brownfield site is redeveloped to its full potential. With assistance from the public-sector, however, numerous projects are able to move forward. Public-sector funds typically support front-end activities such as environmental assessment and remediation, demolition, and site preparation, whereas private-sector funds more often support redevelopment and construction of new facilities. Among the 20 case studies, a variety of public funding initiatives were utilized — ranging from traditional economic development programs, to low-income housing tax credits, to the use of federal Superfund dollars. A brief discussion of these funding initiatives follows.

General Obligation (G.O.) Bonds. Many of the projects described in this book were financed through issuance of bonds, backed by the general obligation of cities or local development authorities. Local governments traditionally issue G.O. bonds for acquiring land, preparing sites, and making infrastructure improvements — key elements in any brownfield redevelopment strategy. Among these case studies, projects backed by G.O. bonds include Scott Peterson Meats and Madison Equipment in Chicago, Illinois, and the Southwest Harbor Redevelopment in Seattle, Washington.

Tax Increment Financing (TIF). Tax increment financing is a system whereby property values in a particular district are frozen at a certain level; when property values rise, the taxes or the increased values are then funneled back into redevelopment projects there. TIFs are built on the concept that new value will be created, and that the future value can be used to finance part of the activities needed now to create new value. The key piece of public-sector financing for redevelopment of Minneapolis' Johnson Street Quarry was revenue from the local TIF district — expected to bring in $10.3 million over the project's life. In Wyandotte, Michigan, city officials financed a portion of the $5.2-million redevelopment at BASF's South Works with TIF district revenues, which, by 1994, provided $5 million annually.

EPA Brownfield Pilot Site Grants. Since its inception in 1994, EPA's Brownfields Pilot Site Program has provided some critical start-up funding for 76 cities and counties nationwide. In Louisville, Kentucky, the city's $200,000 grant was used in part to assess environmental conditions at the Ni-Chro Plating property (a neighboring company sought to purchase Ni-Chro in order to accommodate its business expansion plans). The city's experience at the Ni-Chro Plating site will be used to craft city-wide brownfield policies. In Sacramento, California, EPA Pilot Site dollars are being used to develop the Environmental Oversight Authority, an innovative team that acts on behalf of state and local government officials to oversee and streamline brownfield site activities.

The Clinton Administration in August 1996 announced support for an expansion of EPA grants to communities for site assessment and redevelopment planning, and support for a revolving loan fund to finance cleanup efforts at the local level. The agency estimates that, by the year 2000, the Brownfield Pilot Site Program will result in cleanup at approximately 5,000 brownfield sites in 300 cities.

Community Development Block Grant (CDBG) Funds. CDBG funds, distributed by the Department of Housing and Urban

Development (HUD) to cities according to formula, can be used to finance the rehabilitation of privately-owned brownfield sites. Several communities examined here utilized a portion of their annual CDBG resources to support brownfield activities. The City of Lawrence spent nearly $600,000 in CDBG dollars on the Lawrence Gateway Project between 1994 and 1996. Bridgeport dedicated $2 million of its CDBG funds to launch assessment and cleanup of the area surrounding Westinghouse's Bryant Electric facility.

HUD Section 108 Loan Guarantees. Related to the CDBG program, Section 108 loan guarantees enable local governments to support physical and economic development projects that are too large to finance with single-year CDBG grants. Under Section 108, localities issue debentures to cover the cost of projects, pledging their annual CDBG funds as collateral. Officials in Buffalo, New York, have dedicated $1 million in Section 108 funds for creation of a new parkway in a blighted, industrial section of town. HUD in fall 1996 stepped up its support of brownfield activities by approving a $50-million loan guarantee to the City of Chicago, using future CDBG funding entitlements as collateral.

Federal Superfund Dollars. In Wilmington, Delaware, the state Department of Natural Resources and Environmental Control (DNREC) sought federal assistance in financing site assessment of 70 older industrial properties along the waterfront. DNREC asked EPA Region 3 in 1994 to support this area-wide initiative with allocation of "Pilot Dollars" under the Delaware-EPA Superfund Cooperative Agreement. EPA responded positively and, since then, has committed $250,000-$350,000 per year for brownfield site assessment work. "EPA officials nationwide are looking for direct success stories," says one DNREC official. "They are looking to spend dollars where they can see direct creation of jobs and taxes and, equally important, an improvement to the environment."

State and Federal Transportation Dollars. Several locales profiled in the case studies utilized state highway dollars to finance site assessment and remediation activities. In Lawrence, Massachusetts, the city drew on Massachusetts Highway Department funds to pay for demolition and site improvements at the Oxford Paper site in order to support the new Canal Street Bridge and a traffic interchange. The city also secured $500,000 in enhancement funds under the Intermodal Surface Transportation Efficiency Act to support planning studies for the Lawrence Gateway corridor. In Buffalo, New York, city officials tapped $3.5 million in Industrial Access Program funds, which are administered through the New York Department of Transportation.

Low-Income Housing Tax Credits. Low-Income Housing Tax Credits were authorized by Congress several years ago as an incentive to attract private capital to housing projects developed for low-income residents; in essence, they help minimize investment risk and shore up the investor's rate of return. The Circle F project in Trenton, New Jersey, was partially funded through the use of Low-Income Housing Tax Credits. State officials determined that the building would qualify for $800,000 in these tax credits per year, beginning when the facility opens in 1997 and ending in 2007. Total tax credits over this ten-year period will be $8 million, and the bank that provided front-end financing expects to see a 12 percent yield on its investment.

State Financial Incentives: Tax Credits and Grants. Some states have developed financial assistance mechanisms to encourage the reuse of contaminated industrial sites. In Delaware, for example, a Brownfield Assistance Fund matches private-sector investments for up to 50 percent of site investigation costs, for a total of $25,000 (available to private-sector entities only). Cleanup and redevelopment activities at the old Harlan & Hollingsworth Shipyard in Wilmington, Delaware, were financed through this fund. In addition, Delaware offers a brownfield tax credit to individuals who build or renovate a building located on a brownfield and where new workers are hired. Delaware officials anticipate that the purchaser of the roundhouse property, within the Harlan & Hollingsworth Shipyard, will be able to take advantage of these substantial tax credits and see nearly a 50 percent return on initial investment.

Empowerment Zones and Enterprise Communities: HUD and the Department of Agriculture. Empowerment Zones (EZs) and Enterprise Communities (ECs) are geographic areas targeted to receive special federal treatment and incentives in order to attract private investment and other economic activity. Depending on the plan developed for the area, benefits can include financial, regulatory, and technical assistance. In December 1994, HUD and the Department of Agriculture named 95 Enterprise Communities (65 urban ECs and 30 rural ECs), as well as nine Empowerment Zones (six urban EZs and three rural EZs). Designation brings several benefits to the selected areas, including $100 million in social service grants for each of the urban EZs, $40 million to each rural zone, and $3 million to each EC. EC dollars have been used to finance brownfield activities in, among other cities, Louisville, Kentucky, and Buffalo, New York.

Availability of Private-Sector Financing

A majority of the 20 case studies examined benefitted from some form of private-sector financial involvement. Following are key sources of private-sector support.

Responsible Parties. Prior to redevelopment, some sites were cleaned up by the party responsible for environmental contamination. Remediation of the Bryant Electric Plant in Bridgeport, Connecticut, for example, is being carried out and financed by Westinghouse, which agreed to turn the clean property over to the city for $1. Bridgeport officials, in turn, are financing demolition of the 500,000-square-foot building to make room for a new manufacturing facility at the site. Similarly, the Texaco Tank Farm in St. Paul, Minnesota, was cleaned by Texaco and then sold to the St. Paul Port Authority, which provided site preparation and infrastructure improvements before selling off parcels to interested buyers. In several instances, the responsible party not only financed the cleanup but also chose to redevelop the property (i.e., opted to retain ownership of the land rather than transfer it to a local government entity). In Sacramento, for example, Southern Pacific is financing remediation at its 244-acre rail yard facility and redeveloping the site for a mixture of commercial, residential, and recreational activities.

Purchasers. Some case study projects were cleaned up by the new property owner when a responsible party could not be identified or held accountable, or where the party was financially insolvent. At the Ernst Steel site in Cheektowaga, New York, the Benderson Development Company purchased the property and assumed responsibility for the cleanup. Likewise in Detroit, Michigan, the Acetex Corporation purchased neighboring H&H Wheel's property to accommodate its business expansion and assumed responsibility for remediation in the process. Even where purchasers do not actually shoulder remediation costs, they usually invest money in redeveloping the site (i.e., by renovating or building new facilities).

Commercial Banks. Many banks are reluctant to loan money on brownfield projects until remedial work at the site has been certified as complete, either with a No Further Action letter or a Covenant-not-to-Sue. In Detroit, Michigan, Comerica bank loaned the Acetex Corporation $2 million to finance redevelopment at H&H Wheel, once remedial work had been completed. At the Circle F factory in Trenton, New Jersey, Nat West Bank loaned Lutheran Social Ministries $4 million to finance construction of a seniors' housing complex.

Foundations. Several projects analyzed in this book received funding from private foundations. For example, the Lyndhurst Foundation provided $10 million for construction of the Tennessee Aquarium and Ross's Landing in Chattanooga, Tennessee. In St. Paul, Minnesota, job training for new businesses at the redeveloped Texaco Tank Farm site was financed in part by several area foundations.

In-Kind Work. In an effort to facilitate redevelopment of mill sites in Oregon, one electric utility and several other private-sector entities teamed up and contributed over $100,000 in legal, financial, and administrative services. In St. Paul, Minnesota, at the former Texaco Tank Farm (now the Crosby Lake Business Park), Northern States Power Company installed utility lines at its own expense, and U.S. West strung fiber optic lines at no charge to the developer.

Risk Management and Cleanup

Risk Management (in lieu of risk-elimination) and Cleanup Standards Tailored to End Use

Contaminated industrial sites traditionally have been cleaned according to the most stringent residential standards, such that children could ingest remediated soils. Increasingly, however, states are recognizing that such cleanups are prohibitively expensive and sometimes unnecessary, especially if a site's end use is commercial or industrial. As such, many states now are allowing certain contaminants to be left on-site, provided that the potential for human exposure or environmental harm is eliminated (i.e., by an impervious surface, such as an asphalt covering or a building). Less stringent cleanup levels for commercial and industrial settings usually are accompanied by engineering or institutional controls, such as deed restrictions, to ensure that inappropriate uses (i.e., residential housing) never occur at the site. The Port of Seattle worked with the Washington Department of Ecology to derive site-specific cleanup action levels for soils based on future industrial land use. Redevelopment of the Carol Cable plant in Warren, Rhode Island, moved forward because of a new law that allowed cleanups to be tailored to end use and permitted the use of engineering and institutional controls where contaminants would be left in place.

Use of Innovative Remedial Technologies

Many cities are realizing that immense cost savings can be achieved by implementing creative cleanup technologies. In Lawrence, Massachusetts, for example, a soil vapor extraction system was utilized to treat contaminated soils on-site, rather than sending them off-site for incineration. In Worcester, Massachusetts, officials used ground-penetrating radar to identify the location of underground storage tanks. Remedial costs at the Ernst Steel site in Cheektowaga, New York, were offset by the use of an experimental hydrogen sulfide liquid treatment that immobilized lead in soils — a process that saved the company upwards of $300,000.

Broader Policy Conclusions

Public Dollars Leverage Private Investment

Minimal public-sector investment often leverages private-sector dollars. For approximately $370,000, Chicago was able to demolish an eyesore, clean up environmental contamination, and provide a clean, secure lot for Scott Peterson Meats — a strong neighborhood company — to use for employee parking. The city's commitment gave Scott Peterson Meats the impetus (and its lenders, the willingness) to invest $5 million in the project, which, in turn, led to the hiring of 100 additional employees. Without that critical public funding, local officials feel that private investment in Scott Peterson's project would never have materialized. EPA Brownfields Pilot Site grants also have been instrumental in leveraging both public and private funds.

Brownfield Projects Often Trigger a Ripple Effect of Revitalization

Participants in these 20 case studies unanimously stress the importance of choosing brownfield projects that lead to further development, so that a ripple effect of economic revitalization may occur. This was the case in downtown Worcester, Massachusetts, with development of the Medical City project. In conjunction with other downtown redevelopment initiatives, Medical City has created a domino effect of economic growth over the past five years. "You can't address one isolated brownfield and expect it to survive alone," says the city's Dave Dunham.

EPA's Brownfields Action Agenda is Removing Many Barriers to Redevelopment

In addition to providing pilot site grants to 70 locales nationwide, EPA's Brownfields Action Agenda has worked to remove many barriers commonly associated with brownfield cleanup and reuse. For example, the agency has clarified liability and cleanup issues (e.g., issued prospective purchaser guidance, promulgated an underground storage tank lender liability rule, and drafted soil screening guidance). EPA also has focused on creating partnerships with local and state government by establishing Regional Brownfields Coordinators and assigning agency staff members to cities around the country. In addition, EPA is forging ties with other federal agencies involved with brownfield issues. Finally, the agency has made job training an integral part of its brownfield efforts. EPA personnel, for instance, are working with the Hazardous Materials Training and Research Institute to expand environmental training at community colleges near brownfield pilot communities. In its first two years, the Brownfields Action Agenda has fostered a brownfield-friendly climate at the federal level, which, in turn, has unleashed action and innovation at the local level.

Brownfield Projects Can be "Pilot Sites" for Shaping Broader Policies

Many of the projects described in this book actually were "pilot sites" used to craft policies and strategies for a broader area. For example, in Louisville, Kentucky, lessons learned during cleanup and redevelopment of the Ni-Chro Plating site helped establish policies for Louisville's city-wide brownfield program. Similarly, construction of the federal courthouse in Sacramento, California, has served as a template for policies affecting the remaining 240 acres of Southern Pacific's rail yard, and the first two years of the Oregon Mill Sites Conversion Project will guide future redevelopment at rural mill sites. At both the Oregon and Sacramento projects, "generic remedies" are being formulated for common environmental contaminants — a step that should save time and lower costs for cleanups at similar properties.

The Worcester Redevelopment Authority (WRA) served as an "institutional pilot" for the creation of a regional brownfield redevelopment authority in Massachusetts. Because the WRA so successfully handled the many challenges associated with the Medical City project, the Commonwealth of Massachusetts in 1995 passed legislation establishing a regional body modeled on the WRA — the Central Massachusetts Economic Development Authority (CMEDA) — to oversee brownfield initiatives.

Experience on the Ground May Be Used to Guide Future Brownfield Policies

To effectively shape brownfield policy, it is critical to learn from experiences on the ground — to understand what is needed, what is lacking, and how public funds may best be spent. This requires a constant exchange of information between practitioners in the field and officials in government, a dialogue that demands some kind of forum or facilitating body.

The Brownfields Working Group in Louisville, Kentucky, is a consortium of public-private entities that teamed up to identify and overcome barriers associated with contaminated site reuse. The group is creating a database of brownfield sites, facilitating community involvement in decision-making, and working to streamline a "process" by which sites effectively may be brought back to use. Similarly, Chicago's Brownfields Forum is a broad-based interdisciplinary task force, launched in 1995, that seeks to identify policies to encourage brownfield reuse in the city. Chicago's Forum incorporates lessons learned through the city's hands-on experience cleaning up and redeveloping contaminated sites under its Brownfields Pilot Site Program. At regular roundtable discussions, Forum members offer policy suggestions as well as identify critical information gaps that warrant further research. In this way, Chicago has been able to address immediate needs "on the ground" while also charting sensible brownfield policies for the future. Many other cities across the country have established similar brownfield policy working groups, including Buffalo, New York; Detroit, Michigan; and Cuyahoga County, Ohio.

Although the projects profiled in *Lessons from the Field* differ markedly, several overarching conclusions have emerged. The most important finding is that brownfield cleanup and redevelopment often are not viable without public-sector intervention to alleviate conditions of "uncertainty" surrounding liability, cleanup standards, or regulatory requirements. The case studies reveal that, where government agencies have made a concerted effort to reduce grey areas through legislation or issuance of guidance, more projects are moving forward with fewer complications. Equally important is the public sector's role in bridging financing gaps — a need stemming from the fact that private-sector entities often do not view brownfield initiatives as attractive or viable investments.

Also key are institutional or organizational factors — such as the presence of a local government agency dedicated to brownfield reuse, strong project leadership, or coordination among different government agencies — that ensure brownfield redevelopment occurs in a timely and cost-effective manner. These "soft factors," which can be difficult to pinpoint, frequently make or break a project.

The case studies presented in the next chapter reveal that brownfields can be — and are being — cleaned up and redeveloped around the country. Although the barriers to reuse are substantial, an array of new policies are helping communities simultaneously address environmental contamination and spark economic activity.

CHAPTER 3
Case Studies

BASF South Works
Wyandotte, Michigan

Key Players

- BASF Corporation — company whose property was redeveloped into public recreation facilities.
- City of Wyandotte — local government overseeing project.
- Michigan Department of Environmental Quality — state regulatory agency.

Background and Nature of Problem

Founded in 1853, Wyandotte, Michigan, is a medium-sized city in the Downriver area, an old industrial center south of Detroit. Originally a steel-making town, it became a chemical manufacturing center in the 1890s because of the large salt deposits nearby. Like many such cities, Wyandotte is struggling to make a comeback, and by all indications, it's well on its way. Successful reuse of BASF's South Works site has played an important role in the city's redevelopment.

The BASF Corporation began operations in Wyandotte in 1890. With the purchase of the Wyandotte Chemical Company in 1969, BASF completed its acquisition of properties in and around the city. In the following years, though, the company began to consolidate operations. Most of the smaller properties were sold off to private developers or transferred to the city for public use. Wyandotte's power plant, hospital, police administration building, and public marina are all located on former BASF properties.

The two largest parcels that BASF continues to own are the North Works, a 230-acre site on the Detroit River, and the South Works, 84 acres on the river's Trenton Channel. The North Works, which is BASF's main operation in Wyandotte, employs 950 people in research and development and in manufacturing, primarily for vitamins and plastics. BASF has invested more than $100 million in the last decade for new and expanded facilities and environmental improvements at the North Works.

The South Works was developed for industrial operations beginning in 1895. For the next century, it was home to numerous activities, including organic and inorganic chemical processing, steel making, and shipbuilding. In the 1980s, however, major changes occurred, and BASF actively began repositioning itself in the global market. Company executives recognized that future growth lay not in manufacturing soda ash, sodium bicarbonate, or other bulk commodity products, but rather in specialty items such as plastics, vitamins, and fine chemicals. BASF, as a result, shut down many of its outdated facilities, consolidated operations at its upriver North Works, and began considering the future of its now-defunct South Works.

One of the major issues that company officials had to contend with was environmental contamination from over a century of industrial activity. Indeed, in 1980 the state of Michigan filed suit against BASF, alleging the release of hazardous substances via contaminated groundwater from the South Works to the Trenton Channel. The principle contaminants were mercury, polynuclear aromatics, and chlorinated hydrocarbons. The Michigan Department of Environmental Quality (DEQ) ordered BASF to encapsulate the site with a clay cap (in order to prevent contaminants from leaching into the channel) and forbade future site development.

Meeting the Challenge

The possibility that BASF's prime waterfront location might be fenced off in perpetuity stunned Wyandotte officials, who were in the process of launching a city-wide revitalization campaign and considered redevelopment along the Detroit River to be a critical piece of the puzzle. "The waterfront was taken by industry in the 1800s," says the city's director of community development, Peter McInerney, "but now that industry was receding and the water quality was improving, the concept of reclaiming waterfront areas for public access made a great deal of sense."

For several years Wyandotte struggled to make its voice heard in discussions between the state and the company. However, McInerney explains, "In the early 1980s, the city was not a major player in this partnership. Cities, in general, were not viewed as important. All discussions occurred between the state and the company." City officials persevered and urged the state to consider alternate plans that would allow some reasonable reuse on the BASF site.

After six years of site testing and negotiation, state regulatory officials responded to the city's concerns by approving Michigan's first-ever consent agreement for long-term remedial actions that did not require encapsulation. The consent order, signed in 1986, stipulated that BASF would institute a long-term groundwater treatment plan in order to prevent contaminated groundwater from discharging into the Detroit River. Under this agreement, the contaminated soils would be left in place. The groundwater underneath would be funneled into collection areas, tested, and discharged into the publicly-owned treatment facility for removal of organic constituents. This solution spared BASF the enormous cost of moving and treating tons of contaminated soils, and, more importantly, paved the way for future development at the site.

The consent decree also marked a critical shift in dynamics between the three principle players: the city, the state, and BASF. Since the 1970s, BASF had been fending off criticism about the environmental contaminants discovered at its plants, but now, explains Steve Kitler of the DEQ, the company had an opportunity to "make good on past mistakes." The city's McInerney agrees: "BASF officials began talking; they realized that silence was no longer necessary." A mood of cooperation and partnership developed among the three parties, which continued to flourish during the next ten years. This cooperation is frequently cited by those involved as the single most important ingredient to the project's success.

BASF's South Works in full operation.

In 1986, BASF installed three groundwater-collection systems at the South Works plant. They will continue to operate for at least 30 years, at a cost of around $460,000 annually to the company. When the systems were in place, officials from the city, state, and BASF sat down and began discussing possible future uses for the site. As they explored various commercial, residential, and recreational scenarios, the planners recognized the difficulties of working within the confines of the groundwater treatment structures. BASF was interested in seeing the property developed, but there were nagging uncertainties about whether all environmental risks on the property had been identified fully and assessed.

BASF's new Wyandotte Shores Golf Course (above) Waterfront Park (below).

Because of these uncertainties, BASF in 1990 hired a consulting firm, Environmental Resources Management (ERM), to complete a comprehensive investigation and risk assessment of the site. The entire 84-acre property was gridded out and tested, as if for the first time, but other than two new "hot spots" few significant problems were discovered. ERM determined that recreational uses of the property were indeed feasible, but only if sufficient soil cover was provided to prevent human contact with underlying contamination. With the assessment complete, BASF met early in 1991 with a committee of local leaders selected by the city, as well as the DEQ, and publicly agreed to contribute $2 million toward the construction of a public park on the northern third of the site. This fueled the project's momentum. The city, state, and company then decided to jointly fund a park design by William Johnson and Peter Pollack, award-winning landscape architects from Ann Arbor, Michigan. According to McInerney, Johnson and Pollack did such an excellent job explaining to DEQ why the park presented a safe, sensible reuse of the site, that state approval for the plans took only 15 days — an almost unprecedented turnaround. As designed, the park would include an open amphitheatre, riverfront walkway with observation decks, picnic area, jogging trail, and a rowing club.

In 1992, the city and BASF conducted a series of public workshops to determine how the remaining two-thirds of the site should be used. According to McInerney, the workshops were attended by a broad range of stakeholders, including neighbors from across the site; the DEQ; the city's planning, recreation, and historic commissions; and other city departments. During that summer, discussions focused almost entirely on construction of a nine-hole golf course. A 1993 feasibility study indicated that user fees would allow the course to be self-supporting and also would pay for maintenance and upkeep of the park at the northern end of the site.

The final plan combined the use of a clay cap as an exposure barrier, coupled with a surface drainage system (clay cap contouring with surface water infiltration collection system) to prevent excess irrigation water from overloading the groundwater extraction system. Construction of the park and golf course began together in 1994. More than 600,000 cubic yards of soil were hauled to the site, creating, on average, a five-foot layer between the surface and the contaminated soils underneath. Both projects, which were completed by the summer of 1996, are under long-term lease to the city from BASF.

In September 1995, dedication ceremonies were held for the opening of the golf course and park. Because this was such a visible and successful brownfield redevelopment project, Michigan Governor John Engler attended the ceremony and lent his support. He emphasized how much can be achieved with visionary planning, strong partnership, and long-term commitment.

Regulatory Framework

Cleanup at the BASF South Works site was conducted in accordance with the Michigan Environmental Response Act of 1982, known as the Polluters Pay Law, which sets general guidelines for the cleanup of contaminated sites. This law was amended in 1991 to impose strict cleanup standards and liability on the current and past owners and operators of these sites. The South Works cleanup qualified as an industrial Type C closure, which means the site could have in-place contaminants with an exposure barrier to prevent contact. Type A or B closures require cleanup to pristine or "residential" levels.

Significant amendments, however, were signed into law by Governor Engler in 1995, dramatically changing the state's liability scheme and cleanup standards for contaminated property. The new law offers full liability protection to current owners and operators, and local governments, in some cases, who are not responsible for contamination at the site. Known as "the causation standard," this provision puts the burden on the DEQ to prove that a party *did cause* contamination at a given site, instead of liability automatically applying to any owner or former owner regardless of causation, as per the federal Comprehensive Environmental Response, Compensation, and Liability Act (CERCLA) statute. In addition, the state replaced its previous framework of cleanup standards with use-based criteria. The state is required under the new law to develop numerical standards for residential, recreational, commercial, and industrial property uses. Whereas the old law required risk levels for carcinogens to be 10^{-6} for "residential" cleanups (one additional incidence of cancer per one million people), the new law allows risk levels to be within the less stringent 10^{-5} to 10^{-6} range.

Financing

The cost of building the park was $3.9 million. BASF contributed the first $2 million, and the remaining dollars were committed through state recreation grants. BASF leases the park to the city for $1 per year. Together with other expenses associated with the South Works, such as shoreline maintenance and grounds keeping, BASF spends more than $1.2 million annually at the site.

The nine-hole, par-36 golf course, which covers the remaining two-thirds of the South Works site, cost approximately $5.2 million in public funds. The bulk of this financing came from two sources: revenues from Wyandotte's tax increment finance (TIF) district and the issuance of tax increment bonds. Tax increment financing is a system whereby property values in a particular district are frozen at a certain level; when property values rise, the taxes or the increased values are then funneled back into redevelopment projects there. In 1988, Wyandotte pioneered the use of tax increment financing for primarily residential areas, designating more than 300 city blocks as a Central Development Area (BASF's South Works was included in this TIF district). By 1994, the revenue from the captured value within the TIF district had reached $5 million annually.

Impacts

In the past decade, Wyandotte has made a noticeable comeback, primarily because of the city's revitalization project which began in the 1980s. "First we focused our efforts on improving the neighborhoods, then we focused on reclaiming the waterfront, and now we see the whole downtown area is coming to life," says the city's McInerney, adding, "We had three new coffee shops open downtown in the summer of 1994!"

The city pursued its campaign by acquiring over 500 substandard residential buildings since 1987, approximately one-third of which were large enough to be resold for new home construction. More than 185 new residences have been built in the city since then. Better neighborhood maintenance, new homes, less density, and more open space all bolstered the city's image and morale. The city had acquired a corridor of land between BASF's South Works and the McKinley School neighborhood, which had once buffered neighborhood residents from the hulking industrial facility.

As plans for the golf course solidified, McKinley area residents became more and more eager to connect to the waterfront area, instead of being shielded from it. This prompted city officials to launch an innovative project, dividing their parcel into lots and commissioning developers to build nine, new top-quality Victorian homes. In April 1994, the city sponsored a three-day event, called the "Festival of Homes," which attracted over 6,000 visitors.

Whereas ten years ago there was no new construction in the McKinley neighborhood and home values ranged between $35,000 and $70,000, now home values range from $70,000 to $100,000 and new homes are priced between $150,000 and $200,000.

Lessons Learned

According to participants involved with this project, redevelopment of BASF's South Works was facilitated by the following:

A Strong Public/Private Partnership

This project illustrates the importance of building strong alliances — between private industry, local and state government, and community residents — to facilitate successful brownfield redevelopment projects. The relationship between BASF, DEQ, Wyandotte officials, and local residents evolved gradually, ultimately establishing a foundation of mutual trust and respect. According to the DEQ's Steve Kitler, "There were no slackers in this group." This comfort level among participants resulted in a strong commitment of public and private funds. BASF's initial pledge to donate $2 million for the construction of the park helped get the ball rolling and persuade other investors in both the public and private sector that the BASF projects were worth backing.

Linking the BASF Project to Broader Revitalization of Wyandotte

Another key lesson from this project is that redevelopment initiatives, when orchestrated correctly, often result in a "domino effect" of economic growth. Wyandotte's revitalization initiatives have built upon one other, fueling a momentum that will no doubt continue into the coming years. Some key reasons for the city's success are a dedicated group of personnel, strong marketing strategies for redeveloped properties (spearheaded by the Wyandotte Community Alliance and the Wyandotte Business Association), and excellent public relations campaigns (e.g., the Festival of Homes).

Bolstering a Company's Image through Brownfield Redevelopment

Finally, this story illustrates how much mileage one company can gain from championing a brownfield reuse project. Don Yarborough, BASF's general manager for the Wyandotte site, calls the South Works transformation a pioneer project for urban redevelopment — certainly one of BASF's "crown jewels." The city's McInerney agrees: "BASF wanted to help create an image of this waterfront area as a nice, clean place. They wanted to prove that it's possible to have a beautiful intelligent reuse of a brownfield."

Contacts

Steve Kitler
District Project Manager
Environmental Response Division
Michigan Department of Environmental Quality
(313) 953-1499

Peter McInerney
Director
Department of Community Development
City of Wyandotte
(313) 246-4512

ACETEX CORPORATION
Detroit, Michigan

Key Players

- City of Detroit — local government, project overseer.
- Michigan Department of Environmental Quality — state agency overseeing property transfer.
- Acetex Corporation — purchaser of H&H Wheel's property.
- REUS Team — Detroit's interagency brownfield task force.

Background and Nature of Problem

The Acetex Corporation, founded in 1946, is a Detroit-based company that supplies wiping cloths and uniforms for the Big Three automakers. In the early 1990s, the firm launched a major business expansion within the city. As part of this effort, one of its divisions, the Mechanics Uniform Rental Co., sought to purchase an adjacent property owned by H&H Wheel Service, Inc. The plans by Mechanics Uniform Rental called for demolishing the existing building and constructing a new $5-million distribution facility on the two-acre site. H&H Wheel had sold and warehoused automotive parts at the location since the 1970s, but in recent years its operations had tapered off.

When Acetex executives approached H&H Wheel, they learned that the auto parts company wasn't interested in selling. As is often the case with brownfields, the company was more comfortable "sitting on its property" than facing the possibility that environmental contamination might be discovered during the transaction. The only way H&H Wheel would consider selling was if Acetex made two guarantees: that H & H would be cleared fully of liability or indemnified; and second, that it would not incur any remediation costs at the site. It was clear to Acetex representatives that this deal would not be easy to negotiate.

Meeting the Challenge

In May 1994, Acetex learned of a local interagency body — the REUS Team — that had been created that year to oversee and facilitate brownfield redevelopment projects in Detroit. The Team is comprised of members from the City Departments of Law, Planning and Development, and Water and Sewerage; the Michigan Department of Environmental Quality (DEQ); the Michigan Department of Commerce; and various other associated agencies and departments. The group meets twice a month to discuss brownfield issues and address redevelopment barriers, but its primary goal is to shepherd particular projects through the system — to achieve concrete results. Through the REUS Team, Acetex was able to initiate a series of discussions with state and city officials about acquiring H&H Wheel's property.

"Acetex started off dealing with the mayor's office," says Debbie Fisher with Detroit's Department of Planning and Development. "The mayor's office suggested that they attend a REUS meeting, so they came to a meeting and did a presentation to a group of state and city officials. At that point, we put together a strategy."

Acetex's first task was to gauge existing environmental conditions at the H&H Wheel's site. During the summer of 1994, company representatives were allowed access to the site in order to complete Phase I and Phase II assessments, which revealed hydrocarbons and low levels of metals in soils; the apparent source of these contaminants was a hydraulic lift, an old underground storage tank, and fill material. Officials from DEQ felt that the primary health risk at the site was direct dermal contact with contaminants in site soils. Because Acetex planned to build a facility that would cover the entire site, DEQ determined that the building itself would serve as an appropriate remedy (the building would act as a barrier to soil exposure). Therefore, no cleanup was required. However, DEQ stated that if other sources of contamination were discovered during demolition of the old building, Acetex might have to pay cleanup costs.

With site assessment complete, state officials began negotiating a three-party agreement, called an Administrative Order by Consent (AOC), between DEQ, Acetex, and H&H Wheel. The AOC spelled out required remedial activities and included a Covenant-Not-to-Sue, which would activate upon completion of the cleanup and at the time the property was transferred to Acetex.

The activities required under the AOC involved demolition of the existing facility, completion of the site investigation, and remediation and removal of any "surprise" contaminants discovered during the construction of the new facility. Acetex agreed to remediate the site up to the cost of $200,000 — an amount that DEQ felt would adequately cover cleanup costs. However, if Acetex could not finish remediation for under $200,000, the remaining liability for cleanup would to revert to H&H Wheel. Although it was extremely unlikely that H&H Wheel would ever pay a cent, this open-ended liability arrangement left the company uneasy.

After months of negotiating, and exactly one year after the project was brought to the REUS Team, H&H Wheel finally did agree to the sell the property. Debbie Fisher with the City of Detroit speculates that Acetex officials, having thus far refused to offer H&H Wheel indemnity, changed their minds and assumed full liability for the property (company officials would not comment on this). One month later, however, Michigan's hazardous waste cleanup laws changed dramatically. The new amendments relaxed state cleanup standards which, in turn, had a major impact on Acetex's remediation plans. Under the old law, site cleanups were specified as either Type A (method detection limits), Type B (residential), or Type C (risk-based closure based on the site's end use, either industrial or commercial). Acetex had originally planned to do a Type C or Type B cleanup, depending on the severity of site contamination. Because environmental assessments had revealed only minor contamination at the site, company officials had decided to spend the money needed to meet the more protective, Type B, residential standard.

Yet under the revised statute, Acetex fulfilled the state's new "residential" standard without conducting any remediation at all. Whereas the old law required risk levels for carcinogens to be 10^{-6} for Type B residential cleanups, the new law allows risk levels to be within the less stringent 10^{-5} to 10^{-6} range. The Acetex property already fell within this new range and, therefore, received a clean bill of health from the state. After DEQ issued a letter of closure in September 1995, Acetex officials tore down the old H&H Wheel building and, within months, had broken ground on their new facility.

Regulatory Framework

The Michigan Environmental Response Act of 1982, known as the Polluters Pay Law, set general guidelines for the cleanup of contaminated sites. This law was amended in 1991 to impose strict cleanup standards and liability on the current and past owners and operators of these sites. But additional amendments, signed by the governor in 1995, dramatically changed the state's liability scheme and cleanup standards for contaminated property.

The new law offers full liability protection to current owners and operators, as well as local governments, in some cases, who are not responsible for contamination at the site. Known as "the causation standard," this provision puts the burden on the DEQ to prove that a party *did cause* contamination at a given site, instead of the reverse and typical standard, whereby an owner/operator must prove *it did not cause* contamination to escape liability. In addition, the state has replaced its previous framework of cleanup standards with use-based criteria. The law requires the state to develop numerical standards for residential, recreational, commercial, and industrial property uses. Whereas the old law required risk levels for carcinogens to be 10^{-6} for "residential" cleanups, the new law allows risk levels to be within the less stringent 10^{-5} to 10^{-6} range. The Acetex project, as noted above, fell within the new residential range.

Financing

The Acetex project was made possible by significant public and private investment. From the public sector, the firm got a serious boost when Detroit was named a federal Empowerment Zone (EZ), a designation that brought $100 million in social service and capital improvements funding from various federal agencies. Several local foundations, community groups, and companies followed suit, pledging $1.9 billion over the next ten years to revitalize Detroit. Acetex received $3 million in loans from EZ monies. An additional $2 million was raised by a commercial bank, Comerica Corp., which issued tax-exempt bonds (made possible through the EZ designation). Jon Russell of DEQ commends Comerica for lending on this project but adds, "Comerica probably would have been reluctant to loan the money for a Type C closure, except that Acetex had significant collateral," more than enough to back the loan.

Impacts

Acetex Corporation and its various divisions (including Mechanics Uniform Rental Co.) are an important business presence in the City of Detroit. In 1994, the company had $52 million in revenues, a 20 percent increase from the year before. It currently employs over 450 people, and when the new 100,000-foot distribution facility opens, 100 additional jobs will be created. Clearly, it was important for city officials to do everything in their power to ensure that the needs of Mechanics Uniform and Acetex were met. Irving Laker, president of Mechanics Uniform Rental Co, told a Detroit newspaper that his company had received several offers to move out of state, but, he said, "We're doing very well right here."

Lessons Learned

According to participants involved with this project, acquisition and reuse of the H&H Wheel property was facilitated by:

The Detroit REUS Team

In this example, one company wanted to purchase another company's land, but it needed the city's involvement to make the deal go through. The REUS Team, Detroit's interagency brownfield task force, served that critical role. The REUS Team is a loose, *ad hoc* body that meets on the second and fourth Wednesdays of each month. It has no formal enabling legislation, agreement, or charter; nor does it have a formal set of procedures or requirements. The group is simply committed to crafting flexible and innovative solutions within the confines of existing laws and regulations. Its results thus far have been excellent. Already the Team has facilitated over a dozen redevelopment projects throughout the city. This group is an effective model that other cities, tackling similar brownfield issues, may wish to examine.

Involvement of All Affected Parties

This real estate transaction was delayed because H&H Wheel officials, who had not participated in the negotiations, were concerned that the final agreement did not fully indemnify them. It became clear to DEQ staff, as well as the assistant attorney general, that future negotiations must include all affected parties. The staff time required to develop an individually-tailored administrative order/covenant is too considerable, especially when there is a high risk of the third party withdrawing because of its dissatisfaction over a product negotiated in its absence.

Use of a Standardized Covenant-Not-to-Sue

Although the REUS team helped expedite discussion and decision-making for this project, several other factors stalled it considerably. According to Jon Russell of DEQ, the time and costs associated with closing the deal were overwhelming, largely because Acetex chose to draft its own Covenant-Not-to-Sue instead of using Michigan's "model covenant" as a baseline document. This meant the state had to comb through each paragraph ensuring that key elements were included. Now, Russell says, the state generally won't proceed unless all parties agree to use the model covenant. "That way," he notes, "we don't have to fight to get needed language back in the document; [the parties] have to fight to get things out."

Contacts

Jon Russell
Michigan Department of Environmental Quality (DEQ)
(313) 953-1530

Deborah Fisher
Department of Planning and Development
City of Detroit
(313) 224-6380

Scott Peterson Meats
Chicago, Illinois

Key Players

- Scott Peterson Meats — purchaser of Chicago Motor Coach site.
- City of Chicago — local government overseer.

Background and Nature of Problem

The former Chicago Motor Coach site was one of the first five properties to be enrolled in Chicago's Brownfields Pilot Program. City officials became aware of the site because an adjacent business, Scott Peterson Meats, was interested in expanding its west-side Chicago plant. The company sought to acquire the Motor Coach property and demolish the dilapidated, three-story brick building. On the cleared lot, Scott Peterson would provide secure off-street parking for its employees — something the company felt was critical, and currently lacking, in the neighborhood. However, the firm was understandably concerned about the possible environmental liabilities associated with owning the Motor Coach site, which was heaped with piles of household trash, demolition debris, and used tires. Scott Peterson officials could only speculate about the extent of contamination underneath.

This 1.8-acre site had a long history of industrial and commercial use. The Chicago Motor Coach Company built a large brick structure there in 1924 and used it for nearly 30 years as a trolley/bus maintenance barn. In 1952, the site was transferred to the Chicago Transit Authority, which continued using the building for storage and maintenance. In the mid-sixties, another firm took title and stored its heavy equipment there. Finally, in 1983, the property was bought by a scavenger business, which used the building for illegal waste storage. That owner never paid taxes, and in the spring of 1993, the city boarded up the building and brought the scavenger operation to a halt. In the meantime, the plant had become a prime location for loitering, vandalism, and drug dealing.

Jessica Rio, coordinator of special projects for Chicago's Department of Environment, assisted in the preparation of this case study.

Meeting the Challenge

The former Chicago Motor Coach property had been tax-delinquent for several years when Scott Peterson Meats and the city began working together. The city took control of the site by submitting a no-cash bid for the property. This "tax reactivation" process gave the city exclusive interest in the site and paved the way for environmental investigation, demolition, and eventual cost-recovery (although, in this case, the previous owner had no known assets).

Scott Peterson Meats acquired and demolished the former Chicago Motor Coach building to expand operations and provide secure parking for its employees.

In April 1993, the city hired a contractor to conduct a Phase I assessment, which includes a site investigation and records search to determine the property's environmental history. Several potential hazards were identified, including drums filled with unknown substances, asbestos-containing materials, gas cylinders, lead-based paint, an estimated five underground storage tanks, and stagnant water and piles of garbage in a cellar. During the three months of intensive Phase II investigations, a total of 11 underground "vaults" or storage tanks were discovered, along with a tank of tar that needed to be heated and removed. In addition, the team found 29 drums of waste sludge, 12,500 gallons of oil and water, 12,600 gallons of waste oil/solvent mixture, three drums of hydraulic fluid contaminated with polychlorinated biphenyls (PCBs), and 15 cubic yards of PCB-contaminated soil. During Phase III, the final contaminants were removed, and the site was graded. By May 1995, only 13 months after the project had begun, the site was a smooth, fenced lot that Scott Peterson Meats could use for secure employee parking.

This multi-faceted project required strong cooperation between city officials and the contractor, especially since investigation of hazardous materials took place at the same time as building demolition and remediation. Completing these three tasks simultaneously was complicated by the fact that only properly trained and equipped personnel could come into contact with the site's hazardous materials.

Regulatory Framework

Although this site fell outside of Illinois Environmental Protection Agency's underground storage tank (UST) program (the use of tanks had been discontinued on the site prior to 1974), the site was cleaned up to meet state UST regulatory standards.

The Chicago Brownfield Program, launched in 1993, is administered through an interdepartmental working group that includes the Departments of Environment, Planning and Development, Law, and Buildings, as well as the Mayor's Office. The program is a three-pronged initiative that includes the Brownfield Pilot Program (different from U.S. EPA's Pilot Site Program), the Brownfield Forum, and Brownfield Research. The Scott Peterson site was among the first five sites included in the Chicago's Brownfield Pilot Program, which focuses on tax-delinquent or city-owned sites.

Financing

At the former Chicago Motor Coach site, the city paid for environmental investigation, cleanup, and building demolition. The environmental work totaled around $250,000 in contractor costs. The demolition expenses were only $120,000 due to the salvage value of steel girders and so-called "old Chicago brick." The property will be transferred to Scott Peterson Meats for a nominal fee in winter 1997.

The five original sites in the Brownfield Pilot Program were funded in 1993 with $2 million in general obligation bonds. In March 1996, the City of Chicago received an additional cash infusion — a $50-million Section 108 loan guarantee from the Department of Housing and Urban Development — which will support future brownfield activities. Under Section 108, localities issue debentures to cover the cost of projects, pledging their annual Community Development Block Grant (CDBG) funds as collateral.

Impacts

Because of the city's contribution, Scott Peterson Meats has invested $5.2 million in a new smokehouse on its existing property and has hired over 100 additional employees to date. Company officials are committed to hiring neighborhood residents, and they have worked closely with a city-funded social service agency to screen job applicants. In addition to removing environmental hazards and neighborhood blight, the project means more jobs for the community and a stable business presence in a part of the city that definitely needs it. The ripple effect of this public/private investment already can be seen: City officials say that some neighborhood residents are looking into transforming a small adjacent lot, also tax-delinquent for many years, into a community garden.

Lessons Learned

According to participants involved with this project, redevelopment of the former Chicago Motor Coach site was facilitated by the following:

An Effective Organizational Model at the Local Level

Redevelopment of the former Chicago Motor Coach site involved a complex environmental cleanup, a rigorous testing schedule, and extensive coordination of personnel. That the project was successful — that it was completed in a safe and timely manner — points to the effectiveness of Chicago's model for brownfield project management. Under this framework, the city's Departments of Environment, Planning and Development, Law, and Buildings cooperate to streamline cleanup, demolition, and economic redevelopment activities. When Department of Environment officials had planned a meeting to kick off Phase II of the Scott Peterson project, for instance, the roles for each team member were clearly mapped out and scheduled. This institutional model has proven effective and is now a routine component of the city's Brownfield Pilot Program.

Chicago's Brownfields Initiative

On a broader scale, Chicago's three-pronged Brownfield Initiative — which includes the Brownfield Pilot Program, the Brownfield Forum, and Brownfield Research activities — provides a strong model for shaping sensible redevelopment policies. The Initiative's guiding principle is that policies should be constantly reassessed and altered as new insights are gained. As such, there is a continuous information exchange between the three program components. The Pilot Program has given city officials practical, hands-on experience with the issues and problems connected to brownfield sites.

In 1995, experience from the Pilot Program was brought into the Brownfield Forum — a broad-based inter-disciplinary task force whose mission was to identify policies that would encourage brownfield reuse in Chicago. The Forum included a wide range of stakeholders, including community organizations, developers, financial institutions, and city representatives. Through roundtable discussions, Forum members identified information gaps and concluded that certain issues should be explored further under the "Brownfield Research" umbrella. One research initiative currently underway involves an economic analysis of brownfield projects. City officials already have learned a key pointer: that larger sites are much more cost-effective to clean up and redevelop than smaller sites. This knowledge, obtained through the Brownfield Research project, is easily fed back into the Brownfield Pilot Program so that city officials may choose future brownfield projects more effectively.

Public Investment Leveraged Private Dollars

A final lesson of this project, and perhaps the most important, was that "a little investment can go a long way." For approximately $370,000, the city was able to demolish an eyesore, clean up environmental contamination, and provide a secure lot for the adjacent landowner to purchase. Indeed, the city's commitment to this project gave Scott Peterson Meats the impetus — and their lenders, the willingness — to pour $5 million into site expansion, which, in turn, allowed the company to hire 100 additional employees. Without that critical chunk of public funds, however, private investment in Scott Peterson's project might never have materialized.

Contacts

Karen Gordon
Chicago Department of Environment
(312) 744-8900

Carl Lewis
Chicago Department of Planning and Development
(312) 744-4190

MADISON EQUIPMENT SITE
Chicago, Illimois

Key Players

- Madison Equipment — company seeking to expand its business.
- City of Chicago — local government overseer.

Background and Nature of the Problem

Madison Equipment, a 70-employee firm that refurbishes assembly-line equipment for food service operations, has been located in Chicago's East Garfield Park neighborhood since the 1960s. Over the years, the company has gradually expanded its business — acquiring parcels along three blocks of West Carroll Street — establishing itself as a strong anchor in the community. In recent years, however, the surrounding neighborhood has witnessed serious decline. Although once considered a stable and prosperous area of Chicago, one where industry and commerce thrived amid residential housing, East Garfield Park increasingly is marked by abandoned buildings, empty lots, and widespread crime. Scavengers are active in the area, and illegal or "midnight" dumping is rampant. City officials report that even viable businesses like Madison have had problems. On two occasions, for instance, illegal scavengers cut the (live) high voltage wires at Madison's plant to access the copper wire located inside.

In 1993, Madison Equipment sought to acquire a nearby property that housed an abandoned building, previously owned by an auto parts manufacturer and a toy manufacturer. By acquiring the building, Madison not only would be able to expand its current business, but also would eliminate the eyesore and safety hazards associated with the abandoned structure. The building had been enrolled in the Chicago Abandoned Properties (CAP) program for over a year. The CAP program primarily deals with abandoned residential buildings where the key concerns are demolition and redevelopment, not environmental cleanup. A lawyer involved with

Jessica Rio, coordinator of special projects for Chicago's Department of Environment, assisted in the preparation of this case study.

the CAP program recognized that this property might have some environmental contamination, and flagged it for inclusion in the Brownfield Pilot Program (which focuses on older industrial or commercial properties). The city's Department of Environment was eager to take on the site, recognizing its redevelopment potential. The agency's Karen Gordon noted, "Partnership with Madison Equipment [would] foster a growing employment presence and accelerate physical changes in the neighborhood."

Following minor cleanup, this abandoned building was transferred from the City of Chicago to Madison Equipment, allowing the company to expand operations.

Meeting the Challenge

As city officials prepared to conduct a Phase I investigation of the site, they encountered a bizarre situation. An individual associated with the previous business was contesting the property transfer to Madison Equipment, claiming that he was the rightful owner. Although his claims were eventually dismissed, the individual managed to keep the matter tied up in court for over a year.

When city contractors and brownfield representatives approached the building for the initial Phase I site assessment, they faced multiple hurdles. Homeless people had taken shelter in the building, and the individual who claimed to own the property had blocked the entry with locks and a guard dog. Only after dealing with these obstacles were the officials able to access the site. The Phase I investigation revealed significantly less site contamination than authorities had feared. In the building, they discovered only a limited amount of asbestos-containing materials, a barrel of waste oil, and a flooded basement. The city sewer department tested the water, then permitted its release into the sewer system. After the basement's water had been flushed out, inspectors discovered an underground storage tank, which could be left in place. One waste oil barrel was removed from the site. Satisfied that no significant environmental contaminants remained on the site, the city proceeded to turn the site over to Madison in spring 1995 for $1.00.

The property transfer was finalized when Madison and the city signed a redevelopment agreement outlining expectations that both parties had for each other. The agreement stipulates that Madison will use its best efforts to hire six to eight workers from the federal Empowerment Zone in which it's located, and to ensure that building rehabilitation takes place within two years. In return, the city agreed to provide an environmental risk assessment on the site (already completed).

Regulatory Framework

Madison Equipment applied to acquire the site through the the Chicago Abandoned Properties (CAP) Program, which is administered through the Department of Housing and focuses primarily on residential sites. Because prior industrial activity had occurred at this site, a city attorney re-routed the parcel into the Brownfield Pilot Program, which is more equipped to handle potentially contaminated properties.

The Brownfield Pilot Program is administered through an interdepartmental working group that includes the Departments of Environment, Planning and Development, Law, and Buildings, as well as the Mayor's Office. These institutional linkages, as well as strong ties with community groups and other levels of government, have been key to the success of Chicago's brownfield program. A recurring challenge has been difficulty gaining site access and obtaining legal control of properties. With the help of three city attorneys, specializing in real estate, building and housing, and environmental law, the city has worked successfully to tackle these challenges and facilitate redevelopment.

Financing

The Madison Equipment property was one of five original sites enrolled in the Chicago Brownfield Pilot Program, which was funded in 1993 with $2 million in general obligation bonds. The city budgeted this money for testing the five sites and remediating at least two. Costs associated with Madison Equipment were minimal: $3,000 for a Phase I site assessment, and legal fees to contest the false claim of site ownership. In March 1996, the City of Chicago received an additional cash infusion — a $50-million Section 108 loan guarantee from the Department of Housing and Urban Development — which will support future brownfield activities. Under Section 108, localities issue debentures to cover the cost of projects, pledging their annual Community Development Block Grant (CDBG) funds as collateral.

Impacts

One year after the city transferred title, Madison has spent $180,000 redeveloping the building. The company plans to create a secure, campus-like setting around its operations by closing off one end of the street, forming a cul-de-sac. Contamination on the Madison site was unexpectedly slight, contributing to the overall cost-effectiveness of Chicago's Pilot Program in its first year. Residual funds from the first year's budget then were used to take on more complicated redevelopment projects.

Lessons Learned

According to participants involved with this project, redevelopment of Madison Equipment's site was facilitated by the following:

City Officials Discovered Less Contamination Than They Feared

At the outset, Chicago officials feared that Madison Equipment might prove to be a "worst-case brownfield scenario," in which the high costs for environmental cleanup outweigh the benefits. However, as is the case with many brownfields, the actual contamination discovered was minimal. City representatives learned first hand that fear of the unknown — and presuming the worst in terms of contamination and liability — are among the strongest deterrents to redeveloping brownfields.

Well-Targeted Public Dollars Successfully Leveraged Private Investment

The City of Chicago spent just over $3,000 on site assessment at Madison Equipment's new site. The company, in turn, has invested upwards of $180,000 in the once-abandoned building. According to the Department of Environment's Karen Gordon, the city's investment has truly paid off. "Madison has secured the western tip of the industrial corridor here, and its actions will hopefully serve to attract other businesses," she says. Lenders and investors are now more willing to look at this area, Gordon adds, because the city has committed public money to get the ball rolling.

Contacts

Karen Gordon
Chicago Department of Environment
(312) 744-8900

Carl Lewis
Department of Planning and Development
(312) 744-4190

CROSBY LAKE BUSINESS PARK (Texaco Tank Farm)
St. Paul, Minnesota

Key Players

- St. Paul Port Authority — local redevelopment agency.
- Texaco — owner of the tank farm and responsible party for environmental cleanup.

Background and Nature of Problem

For over 40 years, St. Paul, Minnesota, has been a thriving manufacturing town, anchored by the presence of large corporations such as 3M, Whirlpool, and the Ford Motor Company. Like many cities across the country, however, St. Paul has acquired its share of contaminated industrial properties or brownfields. More than 1,000 acres in the urban area contain some soil contamination that renders them "undevelopable" in their current state. Much of this land sits idle instead of generating local taxes and providing jobs. At the same time, the St. Paul Port Authority, the local industrial redevelopment agency, reports that demand for land in the metropolitan area is quite high. "We don't have enough 'product' to offer our business customers," writes the port authority's Lorrie Louder in the August 1995 *Remediation and Reuse*. "They therefore shop elsewhere. Meanwhile contaminated sites continue to exist and in some cases share their contamination with adjacent properties." The port authority estimates that if the city's 1,000 acres of brownfields were redeveloped, approximately 13 million square feet of new light manufacturing space would be generated, creating over 13,000 jobs and more than $25 million in new annual property taxes.

One brownfield site that the port authority has long sought to redevelop is the 40-acre Texaco Tank Farm, located in a commercial-industrial corridor on the southwest side of St. Paul. Texaco began operating this facility in the early 1960s, but, shortly thereafter, started scaling back its service station holdings in the area. In the 1980s, the company decided to remove from the "farm" its ten large, above-ground petroleum tanks. Several years later,

Texaco and the St. Paul Port Authority initiated talks about the site's future use. The port considered the parcel an excellent location for a new, light industrial park — it was centrally located with access to highways, and had strong neighborhood support for redevelopment — but comprehensive site assessment and cleanup would need to take place before the port could take title.

Meeting the Challenge

In spring 1993, negotiations between the port authority and Texaco intensified. Texaco agreed to work with the port and the Minnesota Pollution Control Agency (MPCA) to remediate the site at its own expense. The property would be the first to proceed through Minnesota's new Volunteer Investigation and Cleanup (VIC) Program. After cleanup, Texaco would sell the clean site to the port authority for roughly fair market value; the port, in turn, would grade the site and provide infrastructure improvements before selling off parcels to businesses. Port officials planned to call the new area the Crosby Lake Business Park after nearby Crosby Lake.

The port immediately began working with the local neighborhood group, called the Old Fort Road Federation. The federation had long been awaiting Texaco's departure, and greeted the port's plans for a business park with intense optimism. To address community concerns, the city downgraded the zoning designation on Texaco's old land from "heavy industrial" (I-3) to "light industrial" (I-1). In addition, the port stipulated that all future development would adhere to the following guidelines: outside storage of heavy materials would be prohibited, setbacks would be required for green space, and no significant noise could be created.

Not surprisingly, the principal contaminant found on Texaco's site was petroleum. Throughout the cleanup process, the company experimented with several different remediation technologies. On the northern portion of the site, Texaco used a "soil washing" technique whereby a machine essentially chews up contaminated soil, washes it, then spits it out "clean" on the other end. According to Roger Johnson, Texaco's area supervisor for environmental services, "This method ultimately was not cost-effective because it required more effort and secondary [remediation] steps in order for soils to meet state action levels." On the site's southern portion, two different approaches were used: soils with minimal contamination were landfilled, while those possessing higher contaminant levels were hauled off-site and treated thermally. Texaco's Johnson explains that under this thermal treatment process, "the soils passed through a kiln, the volatile hydrocarbons were captured, and the clean soil was cooled for eventual return to the Crosby Lake site. Texaco officials have spent at least $1 million on site assessment and remediation to date. They have sunk groundwater monitoring wells throughout the property and plan to continue monitoring for the foreseeable future.

In summer 1994, the port authority encountered what the port's Lorrie Louder calls a "mini-crisis." The contamination discovered on the southern half of the site was much more serious than that found on the northern portion. This meant that redevelopment on the northern parcel was being unnecessarily held up while cleanup on the southern end proceeded. The port solved this problem by dividing the site into two parcels — bifurcating the site — and dealing with them separately. When the northern half was fully remediated, MPCA issued a No Association Letter to the port authority (absolving the port of liability for past contamination) and a Certificate of Completion to Texaco. This arrangement allowed the port to take title of the ten northern acres by fall of 1994 and to proceed with infrastructure improvements, including road building and utilities.

The site grading for the northern parcel was completed and the final cap applied by spring 1996. At that time, the port authority sold the site for $1 dollar to EMC, a company that produces educational materials, which had plans to construct a 120,000-square-foot manufacturing facility. Meanwhile, the port has been working to secure three deals for the 20-acre southern portion of the Texaco site. To date, it has established two purchase agreements. The first is with Summit Brewery, a local micro-brew company, and the second is with Twin City Tile, a company with a long-time presence in the St. Paul area. The third potential purchaser is a large company that is considering moving into the metropolitan area from the suburbs — bucking the typical trend of exurban migration occurring in most cities today. Although the port will sell the Texaco land to purchasers for $1 dollar — certainly a great deal for any incoming company — it also establishes requirements that the occupants must agree to meet. First, at least 30 percent of the parcel must be covered by buildings in order to maximize job creation; second, companies must spend a minimum of $30 per square foot in construction costs (i.e., no shoddy, flimsy construction); and third, 60 percent of any new jobs created by the company's move must be filled by St. Paul residents.

Connecting real estate development with new neighborhood economic activity was one of the port authority's top priorities, according to Louder. To meet the challenge, the port spearheaded an innovative program called the Employment Connection that works with businesses to determine their specific employment needs. It then links up neighborhood groups and creates a customized training package for particular companies. "This program is cutting edge because we get real jobs for real people at decent wages, as opposed to messy job training programs that aren't targeted for specific ends," says Louder. "We're getting great feedback from neighborhoods and foundations." Dick Hanson, vice president of the 3M Foundation, confirms this. His company has allocated $100,000 in the past two years to support job training for 3M vendors — something it has never done before. "It's a great new concept," says Hanson, "a way that the public and private sectors can meet the needs of both growing businesses and unemployed people in St. Paul." Businesses typically kick in 10-15 percent of the costs for the training package, while the remaining funds are provided by the state ($650,000 between 1995 and 1996) and private corporations and foundations ($207,000 in grant money to date).

EMC broke ground for its new manufacturing facility on the northern portion of the site in June of 1996; within the next year, port officials are planning a huge opening ceremony to showcase the other companies locating at the new Crosby Lake Business Park.

Regulatory Framework

Minneapolis and St. Paul were two of the first U.S. cities to establish a policy of redeveloping industrial sites within their boundaries. During the 1980s, sites were purchased through the Minneapolis Light Industry Land Acquisition Program, in which the city accepted responsibility for the property's environmental cleanup costs. Currently, sites are purchased directly by the Minneapolis Community Development Agency (MCDA). The state's Volunteer Investigation and Cleanup (VIC) Program, meanwhile, makes possible a transfer of property to municipalities, private parties, and lenders without a transfer of liability. Thus, the polluter remains the responsible party despite MCDA activity on the site. The MCDA then can pursue reimbursement for cleanup costs from the responsible polluter.

On July 1, 1995, the State of Minnesota, through its Contaminated Sites Cleanup Program, appropriated $7.8 million for cleanup of contaminated sites in an effort to refuel economic development. The money, available through the Department of Trade and Economic Development, is disbursed through competitive grants, which are matched by local funds. Properties are subject to certain eligibility criteria, one being that they cannot have Superfund designation. Three-quarters of these state appropriations have been earmarked for metropolitan cleanup sites, while the remaining fourth is intended for rural and suburban remediation activities. The Texaco Tank Farm site was not eligible for such funding because an identifiable PRP, Texaco, would pay cleanup costs.

To remedy the various problems stemming from the movement of economic opportunity (e.g., housing and jobs) into outer-ring suburbs, the state has levied a property tax on the Twin Cities Metropolitan area, which is expected to generate a fund of approximately $6.8 million per year. This money is being earmarked for site remediation grants to be distributed by the Metropolitan Council. Although no specific criteria were written into the statute, the state now is drafting eligibility requirements. Following the tax collection in 1996, grants will be available to sites in Minneapolis and St. Paul and in the surrounding counties.

Another recently-passed statute directs MPCA to consider the intended use for a redevelopment site when establishing cleanup standards. Perhaps more significantly, MPCA and the U.S. Environmental Protection Agency (EPA) Region 5, in May 1995, signed a Superfund Memorandum of Agreement (SMOA) in which EPA pledged not to pursue enforcement activities at sites that successfully completed Minnesota's VIC program. According to the SMOA, "When a site in Minnesota has been investigated or remediated in accordance with the practices and procedures of the VIC program and the MPCA has issued a no action determination...or a certificate of completion (or an off-site determination), Region 5 will not plan or anticipate any federal action under Superfund law unless, in exceptional circumstances, the site poses an imminent and substantial endangerment or emergency situation." In the past, EPA had promised verbally to honor the state's liability exemption measures, but private parties continued to fear federal involvement. With this clause now in writing, private parties have been more willing to develop contaminated sites. MPCA officials believe this agreements's impact will outweigh the benefits of many brownfield statutes recently passed by the Minnesota state legislature.

Financing

Texaco paid for all site remedial activities, which by fall 1996 totaled some $1 million. The southern portion of the site is still being cleaned. When the northern site was certified complete by the MPCA, the port paid nearly fair market value for the property. The purchase price and infrastructure costs totaled over $6.2 million, for which the port authority floated general obligation bonds backed by the City of St. Paul.

Participating businesses paid for 15-20 percent of the port authority's job training program, the Employment Connection. The remaining money for this program was raised from area corporations, foundations, and the state.

Two companies have provided significant in-kind services at the Crosby Lake Business Park. Northern States Power Company installed utility lines at their own expense, and U.S. West phone company strung fiber optic lines throughout the business park.

Impacts

This project has transformed a 40-acre, defunct eyesore into a productive light industrial business park that the port authority estimates will create 350 new jobs and generate $640,000 in new annual property taxes. Ten of Texaco's 40 acres have been deeded by the port authority to the St. Paul Parks and Recreational Department as part of the Mississippi River Open Space Area.

Lessons Learned

According to participants involved with this project, redevelopment of the Texaco Tank Farm was facilitated by the following:

A Strong Partnership Between the State Agency, the Local Redevelopment Agency, and the Responsible Party (Texaco)

According to Lorrie Louder of the St. Paul Port Authority, the partnership between MPCA, Texaco, and the port was "absolutely critical to the success of this project. It all comes down to a positive relationship between the state agency, the local redevelopment agency, and the business responsible for the cleanup. The MPCA treats local government like a customer; we really get timely responses. The tone of all negotiations was: collectively we have a problem here that we all must solve together." Texaco's Roger Johnson agrees that this partnership has been positive. "The port really was able to help us with local issues [Texaco's regional office is in Tulsa, Oklahoma], with neighborhood concerns, and with state agency permitting," he says. "They have an understanding of the political climate."

The Port Authority: An Effective Redevelopment Agency

The port authority is the industrial redevelopment agency for the City of St. Paul, established by the state legislature over 60 years ago. Staffed with 20 employees, its four principle activities are business park development, industrial financing, technical and customized job training services, and river-related port activities. The agency has taken the lead on brownfield redevelopment projects in St. Paul. "The bottom line is that the port authority is small, focused, and we crank out job creation deals," says the port's Louder.

The Port Authority's Innovative Job Training Program

The port authority's innovative job training program, the Employment Connection, helps link real estate development with neighborhood wealth creation. The port works with businesses to determine their specific employment needs, links up various neighborhood groups, and creates a customized training package for companies. Businesses pay 10-15 percent of the costs for the training package, while the balance is provided by the state and private corporations/foundations. This program helped ensure that new employees hired by businesses at Crosby Lake Business Park were properly and effectively trained.

Contact

Lorrie Louder
Director, Industrial Development
St. Paul Port Authority
(612) 224-5686

NORTHEAST RETAIL PROJECT
(Johnson Street Quarry)
Minneapolis, Minnesota

Key Players

- Minneapolis Community Development Agency — local redevelopment authority.
- Rainbow Foods and Target Stores — largest tenants of the new discount mall.
- Ryan Company — Minneapolis-based developer.

Background and Nature of Problem

Northeast Minneapolis, separated from downtown by the meandering Mississippi River, is home to a largely middle-class, European immigrant population, an area "characterized by a strong sense of neighborhood and community," says Jim White, senior project coordinator with the Minneapolis Community Development Agency (MCDA). One thing this neighborhood never has had is a large full-service grocery store, like the kind increasingly found in surrounding suburbs. "Big grocery stores are not going into the inner city," Council Member Walt Dziedzic told the *Minneapolis Star Tribune* in 1996. "Redlining: that's a concern in the Northeast [neighborhood]." A number of residents without cars must rely on smaller convenience stores that charge top prices for food.

Since the early 1980s, Minneapolis officials have been working hard to attract a full-service grocery store to this part of town. Their efforts have repeatedly failed because of inadequate space for large-scale development and concerns about environmental contamination in downtown areas. In the early 1990s, the Ryan Company, a Minneapolis-based developer, almost clinched a deal with one grocer, Cub Foods, but, at the last minute, the store pulled out to locate in the suburbs. When Ryan asked another grocer, Rainbow Foods, what it would take to open a store in Northeast Minneapolis, the owners replied, "The presence of other big discount stores that will draw a lot of traffic." With this feedback, Ryan contacted the Dayton-Hudson Corporation (owner of Target Stores) and several other discount retailers, including Home Depot. The stores agreed to team up with Ryan to explore building a suburban-sized shopping mall on the site of the defunct Johnson Street Quarry in Northeast Minneapolis. While filling the neighborhood's critical grocery store need, the deal also would achieve environmental cleanup in an area long known to be contaminated.

From 1937 to 1957, the Johnson Street Quarry had been an active limestone quarry and rock crushing operation. The northern half of the quarry was backfilled between 1940 and 1945. During the 1960s, the rest of the quarry was filled with architectural debris from the demolition of the Gateway District, an old "skid-row" area in downtown Minneapolis. Although sporadic development occurred on the site over the next three decades, by the 1990s all that remained was a patchwork of small businesses, several truck terminal buildings, and scattered debris. City officials considered the site to be a blighting influence and were eager to see it redeveloped.

But the old Johnson Street Quarry was plagued with typical brownfield challenges that had stymied reuse initiatives for years. Although the site possessed many attractive qualities — excellent access to the metropolitan freeway system, as well as location within a redevelopment project area and a tax increment financing district — potential developers balked at the site's 60-year legacy of industrial activity. Further disincentives included the high costs associated with site assembly (the old quarry consisted of 12 different tax parcels), demolition of existing buildings, and site preparation. Until Ryan entered the picture in 1993, these barriers were significant enough to encourage developers to locate their projects elsewhere.

Meeting the Challenge

In August 1993, officials from Ryan, the City of Minneapolis, Target, and Rainbow Foods publicly announced their commitment to a Northeast Retail Project. However, it would take almost three more years of negotiation, planning, and community feedback before the project advanced.

The plan was that the MCDA would acquire the proposed site from the current owners (including some reluctant sellers), demolish existing structures, remediate contaminated soils, and grade the site. The assembled and cleared site would then be sold to Ryan and Dayton-Hudson for twice its appraised market value, which, even then, would be significantly less than the public costs to prepare the site. The city hopes to recoup its expenditures within 15 years through property taxes and revenues generated from the tax increment finance (TIF) district.

Tax increment financing is a system whereby property taxes in a particular area are frozen at a certain rate; when property values increase, the margin of increased taxes is funneled back into the district to support redevelopment projects. The quarry site is located within the Broadway I-35W Redevelopment Project and Tax Increment Financing District, which was established by the City of Minneapolis in 1977 to promote industrial development in the area. In August 1993, Minneapolis officials began drafting a new redevelopment and tax increment financing plan that included the Northeast Retail Project, and they created a new hazardous substance subdistrict for the site. In a hazardous waste subdistrict, all tax revenues generated from that subdistrict, including the baseline property value assessment, revert back to the TIF area.

At the outset, MCDA established four concurrent tracks of activity for the Northeast Retail Project.

- **Community Involvement**. The city began working closely with neighborhood representatives and established a task force.
- **Developers**. City officials worked closely with the developers to secure Letters of Intent (their commitment to open stores) and resolve liability questions.
- **Costs and Financing**. The city began assessing estimated public/private costs and exploring financing mechanisms.
- **Environmental Conditions**. The city and developer formed an environmental assessment team and began exploring remediation strategies.

Community involvement was the centerpiece of the Northeast Retail Project. Soon after the initiative was announced in 1993, MCDA assembled a neighborhood task force comprised of two business groups and 14 area neighborhoods. The entire group met monthly in a televised public forum; subcommittees gathered as often as once a week. Meetings of the task force revealed that the surrounding neighborhood had conflicting feelings about the project — while the mall addressed key shopping needs and promised economic growth, it also ushered in new problems. In its May 1994 *Final Report*, the task force wrote, "Neighbors are concerned that building the shopping center will lead to the deterioration of the quality of life in the neighborhood. [It] will be a massive structure that will dominate the surrounding neighborhood. Thousands of people will be attracted to the center daily. [But] shoppers will bring not only their money to northeast Minneapolis. They will also bring traffic, noise, threats to public safety, and pollution." As such, the task force concluded that it *opposed* the project unless 18 minimum requirements were met in the following three categories.

Traffic Control Measures. The city or developer must install traffic control devices, develop a comprehensive traffic management plan, and provide transportation services (to be financed by shopping center merchants and the Metropolitan Council Transit Operation) for area residents who don't have cars.

Economic and Environmental Concerns. The city must work with neighborhood organizations and local businesses to halt the decline of the main Northeast business corridors; suitable alternatives must be found for neighborhoods in the Northeast community that may lose a grocery store as a result of this project; MCDA must try to find satisfactory locations within the city to relocate existing businesses that will be displaced by the shopping center; merchants must enact policies to expedite the hiring of area residents; existing pollution on site must be cleaned up and no new degradation created during construction.

Design. Streets must be repositioned, sufficient berming and landscaping installed, and lighting placed to provide pedestrian safety and to shelter surrounding neighborhoods from the shopping center; noise abatement measures must be installed; berms, bike paths, and walking paths must be constructed; the developers and merchants must meet annually with neighborhood organizations to discuss shopping center problems, plans, and opportunities; the final design of the shopping center must be approved by the neighborhood task force.

When the report was issued, the city and the developers unanimously agreed to meet the task force's stipulations. "There were no surprises on the list," says Jim White with MCDA. "All along, there had been a strong dialogue between the various partners, and we agreed to address the community's concerns point by point." The Public Works Department committed to developing a comprehensive traffic management plan; the stores in the Northeast Retail Center agreed to provide transportation; and the developer, Rainbow, and Target all pledged to hire locally. Because these needs were met, the project obtained strong community support, something that was critical for its overall success.

While neighborhood outreach efforts were underway, city officials began working closely with the developer and tenants. These negotiations continued from fall 1993 until winter 1996. One of the first steps involved the MCDA granting "exclusive rights" to the identified tenants, meaning that other parties would not be considered once the agreement was final. The developer and tenants, in turn, formalized their commitment by signing Letters of Intent with the city. The next task was to resolve liability questions about past site contamination. The Minnesota Pollution Control Agency (MPCA) agreed to issue the MCDA a "no association letter" which would essentially absolve the city and all future landowners of liability for existing contamination. The tenants also wanted to make sure that construction of their portion of the site would not be held up if pollution problems surfaced at another location on the site.

The city, for its part, began to consider how to maximize the project's cost effectiveness. "We knew it would have to be a big enough site to pay back all the public costs for assessment and remediation," says MCDA's Jim White, "so what we did was assemble a group of different properties — some polluted, some not-so-polluted — to defray the overall costs." The city also examined whether commercial activity was, in fact, the best use of the site. At the time, the Johnson Street Quarry was zoned industrial. After conducting a study comparing expected revenues from industrial vs. commercial use, city officials found that a retail development would generate twice the revenues of an industrial operation. With these figures in hand, the city moved ahead with acquisition in January 1996. Most of the current owners did not fight the condemnation, although they haggled over price. (A reluctant seller did, in fact, challenge the condemnation in court, but the judge swiftly rejected the claim and ordered that the land be transferred to city ownership immediately.)

The city hired Peer Environmental and Engineering Resources, Inc. (PEER) to conduct extensive pollution testing at the site. City officials had to establish access to all the properties — something that irked some of the current landowners. Results revealed serious contamination of soils and groundwater (primarily caused by materials disposed of in the quarry), leakage from abandoned drums and underground storage tanks, and surface spills. Contaminants include chlorinated volatile organic compounds (VOCs), polychlorinated biphenyls (PCBs), and petroleum. Methane gas, which migrates and creates hazards for existing structures as well as proposed buildings, is present because of decomposition of the quarry fill material. PEER determined that remedial actions would include the removal and disposal of abandoned containers and drums, in-situ soil venting of deep VOC and petroleum-impacted soils, in-situ stabilization of deep PCB-impacted soils, construction of a perimeter methane venting system, and long-term monitoring of groundwater quality. The MPCA approved a Remedial Action Plan (RAP) for the project in fall 1995.

For areas possessing serious contamination, soils are being excavated and transported off site. Where the state determines that minimally contaminated soils may be left on site, MCDA is using a "dynamic compaction" or "pounding" technique to help seal and contain the contaminants (pavement or structures also will be installed over these areas to eliminate exposure pathways).

In fall 1995, contractual negotiations between the developers and the tenants stalled over a few legal issues — a delay that posed a serious problem for the city since the neighborhood's TIF district, which was providing the key piece of public financing for the project, was due to expire in 2002. Without at least five years of revenues from the TIF district — between 1997 and 2002 — the financing for the deal was in jeopardy. "Every month that the project didn't go forward, the city was losing $134,000 in money from the TIF district," says White. In fact, project participants resolved their legal issues only one half hour before a City Council meeting at which MCDA's White was planning to announce that the deal was dead.

Final site plans for the Northeast Retail Project call for 420,000 square feet of retail space. Shops include Rainbow Foods, Target, Home Depot, PetSmart, TCF Bank, an office supply store, and three other regional or national discount specialty retailers. The City of Minneapolis had acquired all the properties by May 1996 and immediately began $7.5 million in remediation and site preparation activities, which continued over the summer and fall. The parcel was turned over to Ryan and Dayton-Hudson in December 1996 for $7.3 million. Construction began right away, and the shopping center is scheduled to open in 1997.

Regulatory Framework

Minneapolis and St. Paul were two of the first U.S. cities to establish a policy of redeveloping industrial sites within their boundaries. During the 1980s, sites were purchased through the Minneapolis Light Industry Land Acquisition Program, in which the city accepted responsibility for the property's environmental cleanup costs. Currently, sites are purchased directly by the MCDA. Through the state Voluntary Investigation and Cleanup (VIC) Program, a transfer of property without a transfer of liability is possible. Thus, the polluter remains the responsible party despite MCDA activity on the site. The MCDA can then pursue reimbursement for cleanup costs from the responsible polluter. Under the VIC program, municipalities, private parties, and lenders are given this liability protection.

On July 1, 1995, the State of Minnesota, through its Contaminated Sites Cleanup Program, appropriated $7.8 million for cleanup of contaminated sites in an effort to refuel economic development. The money, available through the Department of Trade and Economic Development, is disbursed through competitive grants, which are matched by local funds. Properties are subject to certain eligibility criteria, one being that they cannot have Superfund designation. Three-quarters of these state appropriations have been earmarked for metropolitan cleanup sites, while the remaining fourth is intended for rural and suburban remediation activities. In February 1996, the Northeast Retail Project received a grant of $1,482,300 from this pool of money.

To remedy the various problems stemming from the movement of economic development (e.g., new housing and new jobs) into outer-ring suburbs, Minnesota has levied a cleanup/redevelopment tax on the Twin Cities metro area. The property tax creates a fund of approximately $6.8 million per year, which is intended for site remediation grants to be distributed by the Metropolitan Council — the public corporation that oversees water, sewage, and regional planning for Minneapolis and St. Paul. Although no specific criteria have been written into the statute, eligibility requirements are being developed. Following the tax collection of 1996, grants will be available to sites in Minneapolis, St. Paul, and the surrounding counties.

A new state statute recognizes the intended use of a redevelopment site when judging cleanup standards. Although the MPCA had considered such factors in the past, the issue of "how clean is clean" is now determined in light of future site use.

In May 1995, MPCA and the U.S. Environmental Protection Agency (EPA) Region 5 office signed a memorandum of understanding that exempts purchasers of cleaned-up sites from any past liability on the federal level once Minnesota has issued a Certificate of Completion, a Letter of No Further Action, or a Letter of No Association. Although EPA previously had promised verbally to honor the state's liability exemption measures, private parties continued to be suspect of EPA intervention. With this clause now in writing, private parties have been more willing to undertake the development of contaminated sites. MCDA's Jim White stresses that company attorneys "always seem to have liability on their mind, and won't sign off on any deal that [implies] liability." MPCA officials believe this agreement's impact will far outweigh the effects of various statutes recently passed in the Minnesota state legislature.

Financing

Project costs are expected to total around $58 million. The bulk of financing, upwards of $32 million, will be generated by private-sector investment. The remaining $26 million will be drawn from a range of local and state sources. The main source of public funds will be revenues generated within the city's TIF district and the hazardous substance subdistrict (officials expect a significant increase in property values because of the new shopping center). One nearby community, Logan Park, has allocated $1.5 million to the Northeast Retail Project from its Neighborhood Revitalization Program — whose funding is generated through TIF revenues from that neighborhood.

In the past year, the City Council has steadily increased the project's public-sector expenditures from $24 to $26 million, due to the discovery of more pollution than was originally anticipated. The main expense — nearly $15 million — is for acquisition of properties from current owners, relocation of those businesses, and demolition.

In February 1996, the Minnesota Department of Trade and Economic Development awarded the City of Minneapolis a $1,482,300 grant under its Contamination Cleanup Grant Program, an initiative that helps put dormant land back on city tax rolls. This program offers financial assistance to applicants that want to remediate contaminated property, thereby encouraging economic growth in areas hindered by pollution. In this case, the grant provided a key piece of funding for the pollution cleanup from the former Johnson Street Quarry.

Northeast Retail Center Budget
(as of June 1995)

REVENUES	
Tax Increment and Hazardous Substance Subdistrict Taxes	$10,357,000
Land Sale Proceeds	7,300,000
Minnesota State Aid (for roads)	1,750,000
MCDA 1991 Transition Money Match	1,733,000
Neighborhood Revitalization Program (Logan Park)	1,500,000
Special Owner Payments	1,500,000
Special Assessments on the Shopping Center	260,000
Minnesota Dept. of Trade and Economic Development Grant	1,482,300
Total	**$25,882,300**
EXPENDITURES	
Acquisition, Relocation, Demolition	$14,210,000
Pollution Cleanup	$2,600,000
Soil Correction	$3,100,000
Highway Access	$1,480,000
Public Improvements to and Along 18th Street	$530,000
MCDA Administration	$500,000
City Fee	$630,000
Contingency	$1,350,000
Total	**$24,400,000**

Impacts

The public benefits that officials expect through this project include pollution cleanup, job creation (1,700 full and part-time jobs), blight elimination, and tax base enhancement (both property and sales tax). Another public goal that will be attained is neighborhood stabilization of Northeast Minneapolis through the provision of essential retail facilities in these poorly serviced communities.

Lessons Learned

According to participants involved with this project, redevelopment of the old Johnson Street Quarry was facilitated by the following:

Strong Relationship Between State Agency and Other Redevelopment Partners

Jim White, senior project coordinator for the Northeast Retail Center, believes that a strong relationship between state personnel and other project participants was one of the key aspects in this deal. "The state was a dream to work with," says MCDA's Jim White. "Developers and tenants always want to know how a state is going to treat them; they certainly found a great deal of comfort with our state agency." There was a constant flow of information between all parties involved. "We were open about our needs, costs, and concerns," White adds. "When questions came up, we'd get on the horn right away with our state personnel." Among the participants emerged an atmosphere of cooperation, rather than mistrust, which helped expedite decisionmaking and reduce costs associated with the project.

Involvement of the Neighborhood from the Outset

Because the community was so involved with every aspect of decisionmaking for this project, the Northeast Retail Project seemed to be an extension of the neighborhood's vision rather than an externally-introduced plan. This, says Jim White, was critical to the project's success. "If they think it's some faceless, unknown bureaucrat pushing the deal through, the neighborhood is going to reject it outright," White explains. "We were trying to get everyone's buy-in. If they [neighborhood residents] had indicated that it was a bad idea, we certainly would have backed off."

White emphasizes the importance of maintaining diligent records of all meetings. For this project, MCDA videotaped all proceedings so no one could argue about what was said or promised — everything would be on tape for years to come. He states that this recording is especially important for projects that take a long time to finalize.

Contacts

Jim White
Senior Project Coordinator
Minneapolis Community Development Agency (MCDA)
(612) 673-5170

HOLDEN-LEONARD MILL
Bennington, Vermont

Key Players

- Vermont Economic Development Authority — state economic development agency.
- Southern Vermont Development Council — local community development organization.
- Mace Securities International, Corp. — corporation now leasing the Holden-Leonard Mill, with the intent to purchase the property.
- Vermont Agency of Natural Resources, Department of Environmental Conservation — state environmental agency.

Background and Nature of Problem

Between 1865 and 1949, the Holden-Leonard Mill complex played an integral role in the industrial and economic development of Bennington, Vermont. During these years, Bennington was the hotbed of southern Vermont's textile industry, with the Holden-Leonard Mill employing one-quarter of the town's workforce. In recent years, however, this town of 16,400 residents has fallen on hard times as many small mills and businesses have closed their doors. In only one year, between 1989 and 1990, the area lost 444 jobs.

In 1986, the Southern Vermont Development Council (SVDC), a newly created, nonprofit community development organization, bought the defunct Holden-Leonard Mill in an effort to spur local revitalization. SVDC planned to purchase the facility for $360,000 and conduct $2 million worth of remodeling in order to create industrial condominiums. To help finance the deal, SVDC borrowed $1 million from the Vermont Economic Development Authority (VEDA), a state economic development agency backed by the state treasury, and another $1 million from the federal Economic Development Administration (EDA). VEDA held the first mortgage on the mill, meaning that if SVDC defaulted on loan payments, VEDA — not EDA — would have first right to foreclose. Several other local and regional development groups loaned a total of

$400,000 on the project. Renovations were finished on the Holden-Leonard Mill in July 1989, and SVDC was scoping out potential buyers when the U.S. Environmental Protection Agency (EPA) halted the proceedings, alleging the presence of hazardous contamination on the site.

SVDC was devastated by this turn of events. A year before SVDC acquired the site, the state Department of Environmental Conservation (DEC) had issued a recommendation of "no further action" to EPA following a state-ordered and supervised removal of process chemicals, chemical containers, and spent petroleum products. According to Paul Bienvenu, then-executive director of SVDC, "We made the appropriate inquiry and relied on the assurance of the appropriate state agency that the site was clean." In other words, SVDC bought the property without conducting its own environmental audit — a not uncommon practice during the early and mid-1980s. DEC officials, however, argued that SVDC should not have assumed that the site was clean based solely on their determination. The DEC's Dave Shepard pointed to disclaimers in correspondence with SVDC stating that DEC's recommendation was based only on what it discovered. When agency personnel had surveyed the site, they found no visual evidence of dumping or soil contamination and, therefore, did not order the responsible parties to conduct soil sampling. "If we came across the same situation today, there would probably be soil sampling involved," says Shepard.

EPA's soil tests revealed elevated levels of heavy metals and polycyclic aromatic hydrocarbons (PAHs), the residue of incompletely burned coal tar and other materials. The agency informed the SVDC that PAH levels were high enough to make the site eligible for the National Priorities List (NPL), a list of the 1,300 most polluted sites in the federal Superfund program. With $2.4 million in public funds already sunk into the mill, SVDC was desperate to salvage the project. The group attempted unsuccessfully to pursue a "de minimus settlement" with EPA in order to limit its financial responsibility for the cleanup, arguing that it did not cause or contribute to the contamination and exercised "due diligence" before the purchase. "The EPA has encumbered our property by virtue of its finding that the property is eligible for NPL proceedings," said the SVDC's Bienvenu in 1992, "and there appears to be no mechanism for releasing that encumbrance."

The site remained on EPA's database of Superfund sites — called the Comprehensive Environmental Response Compensation and Liability Information System (CERCLIS) — for nearly eight years, a status that cast a pall of uncertainty over the project, warding off potential buyers and lenders. Any company that purchased a portion of the mill would have entered into the chain of liability and assumed responsibility for environmental contamination. The mill, therefore, remained vacant for several years, and its owner, SVDC, soon began defaulting on loan payments. "In fact, the big loan went south almost immediately," says Paul Denton with VEDA. "It was a huge black eye for VEDA." SVDC dissolved shortly thereafter.

Meeting the Challenge

The logjam was broken in 1992 when Mace Securities International (MSI) Corporation expressed an interest in buying the mill. MSI develops, manufactures, and markets personal security products and is a well-known supplier of non-lethal self-defense sprays to civilians and law enforcement officials. For several years, the company had occupied the building next door and now was interested in moving its headquarters into the Holden-Leonard Mill, hiring several hundred new employees in the process. MSI would not consider the deal, however, until all environmental concerns at the site were resolved.

At this point, VEDA stepped up to the plate. "We realized that the site wasn't going to get any better until somebody really owned it and took responsibility for it," says VEDA's Denton. "And the bottom line is, we had all the problems associated with owning the buildings and none of the advantages."

In February 1993, VEDA finally moved to foreclose on the property, essentially removing it from SVDC's possession. One month later, the mill was sold off at a court-ordered auction, at which VEDA was the sole bidder. The group successfully acquired the 20-building complex for a $1.5 million "credit bid," meaning that it bought the mill for the amount it had lent on the project during the past eight years — $1 million — plus roughly $500,000 in accumulated interest. None of the other lenders, including the federal EDA or the Town of Bennington, saw their money again. But Bennington officials argue that if the venture with MSI succeeds, their investment will have been worthwhile.

VEDA planned to lease the building to MSI while EPA and the DEC continued investigating site contamination. Once environmental cleanup was complete, VEDA would sell the complex to MSI for approximately $1 million. In August 1994, a lease agreement was signed between VEDA and MSI — the first step towards transferring the mill to MSI. At that time, the company made a "good faith deposit" of $150,000 toward the property's purchase price and began leasing the building for $48,000 annually. In the next three years, the company spent nearly $500,000 to refurbish the mill, redesign interior spaces, and install new wiring and piping.

As of fall 1996, VEDA and MSI were in the advanced stages of negotiating, but some environmental questions remained. The Vermont Department of Health was evaluating additional tests that had been conducted by DEC during the previous year. Bruce Linton, site project manager for DEC's Division of Waste Management, says, "There are preliminary indications that some risk may exist requiring remediation, such as grading, capping, and paving." Once these issues are resolved, MSI will consider taking title. "We have to prove to [MSI officials] that there are no environmental problems at the site, otherwise they'll just go on leasing the building forever," says VEDA's Denton. Not that that option would be the end of the world. "Our objective," he notes, "is to create an atmosphere where jobs can be created, so whatever keeps them happy and growing in that building in Bennington — that's what counts."

Another key factor stalling the real estate transaction has been EPA's continued involvement with the site. For eight years, the Holden-Leonard property was one of 1,200 New England sites being evaluated by EPA for inclusion on the NPL — a status that stigmatized the property because of Superfund's reputation for being costly, time-consuming, and administratively daunting. Fear of Superfund, says DEC's Bruce Linton, means that "a lot of site owners would rather deal with [the state agency] than EPA." Responding to these concerns, EPA in recent years has moved to streamline the Superfund program by handing over more responsibility for site cleanup to states. In 1995, the agency released over 25,000 minimally contaminated sites — designated No Further Remedial Action Planned (NFRAP) — from the CERCLIS database, delivering them into state hands. In 1996, EPA's Region 1 office (New England) took an additional step of relinquishing to states oversight of certain *non*-NFRAP sites (i.e., ones still under federal assessment). The Holden-Leonard Mill was one the first of these non-NFRAP sites to be granted state oversight.

This move was prompted by an April 1996 letter from Vermont DEC to EPA Region 1, requesting that a "comfort letter" be issued to VEDA. The state argued to EPA that the Holden-Leonard Mill would best be managed by the DEC for these reasons: (1) Serious site contamination had not been discovered; (2) a viable responsible party (VEDA) was cooperating fully with all state requests; and (3) the state had the ability (in terms of personnel, resources, and expertise) to oversee the site. Equally important was the fact that a solid prospective purchaser, MSI Corp, was in the picture. Within five weeks, EPA responded by issuing VEDA a "comfort letter" stating that no further steps would be taken to list the site on the NPL. In its correspondence, EPA wrote: "Our goals are to focus federal resources where they are most effective, encourage private party responses under state authorities, reduce duplicative efforts due to overlapping state and federal requirements, and provide the public with an opportunity to review and comment on site priorities and actions." By all indications, EPA's release of the Holden-Leonard Mill will be a key step in expediting the transfer of this property from VEDA to MSI Corp.

Regulatory Framework

Vermont's Contaminated Properties Redevelopment Program, signed into law in spring 1995, began accepting applications for participation on January 1, 1996. The program is designed to handle low-priority sites that would otherwise go unnoticed by the state. Vermont operates an Underground Storage Tank program rather than a state Superfund program, since 87 percent of its hazardous waste sites are from leaking underground petroleum tanks. Vermont's environmental enforcement officials historically have worked to remediate the remainder of the state's hazardous waste sites under the direction of the federal government.

Under the new law, third parties, or prospective purchasers, may seek liability relief following successful corrective action at eligible sites. The DEC's Hazardous Materials Management Division maintains oversight authority throughout the cleanup, including approval of site investigation work plans, on-site sample collections, corrective action work plans, and the corrective action itself.

Cleanup standards associated with Vermont's Contaminated Properties Redevelopment Program are the same as those required under other DEC programs. Cleanups must comply with Vermont's Groundwater Protection Rules, which are currently under revision and slated to be finalized by spring 1997. The state has no soil cleanup standards at this time and instead relies on EPA Region 3's Risk-Based Tables for contaminated soils, as well as an interim soil guidance document that is based in part on the state's groundwater standards. Generally, cleanups are done on a site-by-site basis with oversight by the state.

An initial application fee is required for DEC review. Following acceptance into the program, participants make a $5,000 deposit, from which costs are drawn. The state may recover additional costs for future oversight. Also the state reserves the right to pursue cost recovery from responsible parties associated with the site. Following a successful site investigation and cleanup, the DEC issues to the third party prospective purchaser a Certificate of Completion, which releases that party from liability for the identified contamination (re-openers exist if additional contamination is subsequently discovered on the site).

Financing

Redevelopment of the Holden-Leonard Mill was financed primarily with public funds. The principal agencies that loaned money were VEDA and EDA. VEDA is a state development agency that draws funds through legislative appropriations, industrial revenue bonds, or monies borrowed from the state treasury. Funds used for the Holden-Leonard Mill were from this latter category. VEDA loaned $1 million and held a first mortgage on the site; when SVDC defaulted on loan payments, VEDA had first right to foreclosure. The agency proceeded to take title to the mill through a $1.5 million "credit bid" (the amount of its loan plus $500,000 in interest) and then moved to sell or lease the facility.

Several other entities loaned on the project, but were never repaid by SVDC. The EDA loaned SVDC $1 million; the non-profit Economic Development Corporation loaned $450,000; the Town of Bennington contributed $25,000; the Bennington County Industrial Corporation loaned $125,000; and a New York construction firm completed over $1 million in mill improvements, but never saw payment for $200,000 of the work.

Other than investments from MSI and the New York construction firm, there was no private money spent on the Holden-Leonard Mill redevelopment. "It simply wasn't financable in the private sector," says VEDA's Paul Denton. "Too risky, no bank would look at it. And that's not just because of environmental concerns. There was just no guarantee that the project would bring a healthy return."

Impacts

There were several years when it seemed as though Bennington's grand Holden-Leonard Mill would never be revived. But since 1993, when VEDA initiated foreclosure and MSI moved into the building, the mill has made a comeback. This, in turn, has meant good news for Bennington. MSI not only has hired over 200 new employees, but it has made significant improvements and renovations to the historic building.

Bruce Linton, site project manager for DEC's Division of Waste Management, anticipates that final sampling results may indicate the need for site remediation. When cleanup is finished, however, the transfer of property from VEDA to MSI should proceed smoothly. The state plans to provide VEDA and MSI with a written response indicating that the cleanup has been completed according to a state-supervised plan. The expectation, then, is that MSI and its jobs will remain in Bennington.

Lessons Learned

According to participants involved with this project, redevelopment of the Holden-Leonard Mill was facilitated by the following:

Strong Public/Private Partnership

The strong public/private partnership between VEDA, the state Department of Environmental Conservation (DEC), and MSI has been key to this project's success. In particular, VEDA officials note that DEC's assistance (and timeliness) in all site assessment and remediation activities has been invaluable. "If I was going to hire someone to be my customer service representative in the private sector, I'd hire the folks from DEC," says VEDA's Denton.

Vermont's 1995 Brownfields Law

Redevelopment of the Holden-Leonard Mill came to a standstill when hazardous waste was discovered after SVDC purchased the site in 1986. At that time, there was no state law in place to encourage voluntary cleanup of brownfields. Vermont's Contaminated Properties Program, enacted in 1994, brings much needed closure to the process by offering third parties or prospective purchasers liability relief upon completion of an approved cleanup plan. "This is a very good law," notes VEDA's Denton. "If you come up with a plan to remediate a property, you can be relieved of liability — a critical step in moving things forward."

Transfer of the Holden-Leonard Mill from EPA's CERCLIS to State Control

In April 1996, the Vermont DEC requested that EPA Region 1 transfer the Holden-Leonard Mill (an active CERCLIS site) from federal to state control, arguing that the state could oversee the remedial process more effectively. One month later, EPA agreed to do so, issuing VEDA a "comfort letter" that marked the end of EPA's involvement with the site (although the state may refer the site back to EPA if the responsible party does not cooperate). This was the first time EPA Region 1 had released from the CERCLIS a Vermont site that was not designated "no further action remedial planned" or NFRAP.

In correspondence to VEDA, the agency wrote, "EPA is now considering alternatives that will make it possible for the states and EPA to agree on a significantly reduced number of sites which are appropriate for the NPL." EPA's policy shift — a willingness to transfer these moderately contaminated sites into state hands — will facilitate redevelopment of brownfields in two key ways. First, it will remove the stigma of federal Superfund designation that has historically warded off investors and prospective purchasers from these sites. Second, because states are closer to their constituents and more familiar with particular sites, it is likely that assessment/cleanup activities will proceed faster and more cost-effectively under state supervision.

Contacts

Steve Greenfield
Vermont Economic Development Authority
(802) 828-5459

Bruce Linton
Site Project Manager
Division of Waste Management
Department of Environmental Conservation
Vermont Agency of Natural Resources
(802) 241-3872

THE FALLON/ST. VINCENT "MEDICAL CITY"
Worcester, Massachusetts

Key Players

- Worcester Redevelopment Authority — local redevelopment agency.
- Massachusetts Department of Environmental Protection — state regulatory agency.
- Fallon Foundation — the hospital complex relocating in downtown Worcester.

Background and Nature of Problem

For over a century, the City of Worcester's economy was supported by heavy manufacturing and its associated industries. In recent decades, however, changing global markets have triggered a shift towards light manufacturing and technology-based enterprise. Many of the old Worcester factories and plants now lie vacant and underutilized, a grim reminder of a once thriving economy there. These abandoned sites neither contribute to the local economy nor yield sufficient tax revenues to support municipal services. Poverty rates in the neighborhoods surrounding these industrial facilities range between 15-35 percent — two to three times above the state average. City officials recognize that this manufacturing decline, and the attendant increase in idle land, have a profound impact on the Worcester economy. As a result, they have worked hard in recent years, along with state agencies, to craft policies that encourage redevelopment of these underutilized sites.

In 1992, the city encountered one of its biggest brownfield challenges to date. That year, two of the largest health care providers in Worcester merged with the hope of building a new $200-million integrated health facility downtown. The new corporation, managed by the Fallon Foundation, consisted of the Fallon Clinic, Inc. (a multi-specialty group practice), the Fallon Community Health Plan (a federally-qualified HMO), and the St. Vincent Health Care System (including the St. Vincent Hospital, Home Health Care, and Providence House Nursing Homes). The new health facility would be called the Fallon/St. Vincent Medical City, or simply "Medical City."

Based on plans for the merger, the Fallon Foundation began looking for a suitable site within Worcester city limits, but corporate officials soon realized that the only parcels available downtown were either riddled with environmental contamination or too small for the hospital's needs. Their search quickly expanded to lands in suburban and rural "greenfield" areas. This served as a wake-up call to Worcester officials, who were intent on attracting the hospital complex as part of their downtown revitalization effort. If built, Medical City would be the first provider of complete medical services — ranging from home health care and fitness programs to the most sophisticated medical and surgical specialties — located in central Massachusetts. The complex was slated to bring in millions of dollars each year for the city through tax revenues, jobs, and related benefits.

Meeting the Challenge

The first thing that city officials did was to identify properties downtown that might be suitable, and then work backwards through the various difficulties. They focused on a 24-acre area, comprised of 32 separate parcels and eight roadways, that was located in a blighted Worcester neighborhood near Interstate 290. This area contained several abandoned industrial and commercial businesses, low-income service providers (e.g., the Salvation Army), and scores of empty lots. Former industrial activities in the 24-acre area included oil manufacturing, electroplating, and a few gas stations. The area was contained in the East Central Urban Renewal Area — an economic opportunity zone that had been established 25 years earlier but had not achieved meaningful revitalization. The city determined that it would be feasible to acquire parcels by eminent domain, initiate cleanup and site preparation activities, and then turn over the property to Fallon within three to four years. With this plan sketched out, officials turned their efforts towards mobilizing the necessary personnel and exploring public financing options.

At the outset, city officials recognized that they lacked the institutional framework needed to effectively manage this project (and brownfield projects, in general). Brownfields initiatives require involvement by a wide range of specialists — including engineers, planners, lawyers, toxicologists, financial experts, and community development experts — most of whom work in different city departments. This fragmentation can frustrate efforts to collaborate and effectively manage projects. Worcester officials tackled this problem by resurrecting and reforming an old quasi-local government agency, the Worcester Redevelopment Authority (WRA), which had been in existence since the 1960s but had played only a minor role in recent development initiatives. In 1992, the WRA was reorganized, granted "independent status" from the city, and staffed with 12 employees whose primary mission was brownfield cleanups and redevelopments. The WRA provides a contrast to traditional planning departments, which, says WRA's Dave Dunham, "might be focusing on 50 different projects, many unrelated to brownfields."

Aerial view of 24-acre area in downtown Worcester where Medical City will be located.

The project's next critical task was to secure solid public financing. The WRA was able to raise $42 million by asking the city to issue bonds; payment of long-term bond interest ($30.2 million over the next 20 years) will be split between the city and state.

As required by Chapter 121B regulations, administered by the Massachusetts Executive Office of Communities and Development, the WRA formed a Citizen's Participation Committee. The group's role was to assess the economic and community benefits of the project (i.e., to determine if it met Worcester's urban renewal objectives and made financial sense, and if so, what short- and long-term resources would be needed). The group consisted of city officials, local business people, environmental groups, historic preservation interests, the Chamber of Commerce, and community advocates. Monthly meetings were held for one year, at the end of which the committee gave the project a green light, and the WRA and Fallon began preparing environmental impact reports. For the next 18 months, another community group — the Citizen's Advisory Committee, formed under the Executive Office of Environmental Affairs (EOEA) — tackled technical and planning questions: Was the proposed site design acceptable? Were community needs being adequately addressed? Were environmental assessment and cleanup strategies sufficient?

The hospital design plans underwent fundamental change based on the community's input. For example, the complex's main entrance was moved from the property's east to west side so that the facility would interact more closely with downtown pedestrian areas. The idea was to create a "golden triangle" of public space between three main structures in the downtown area: the convention center, the Worcester Common Fashion Outlet, and Medical City. In summer 1993, the city hosted a three-day "Urban Design Charrette" to further encourage public participation in the design process. Plans called for a 675,000-square-foot complex comprised of the hospital and medical offices, an atrium entry, retail stores, structural parking, and a free-standing energy plant.

In 1992, Medical City was designated a "Major and Complicated Project" by the Massachusetts Secretary of Environmental Affairs, under the state's Environmental Policy Act. This designation means that, although the site has complex environmental challenges, the state feels there are strong incentives for redevelopment and therefore agrees to commit extra measures of support. To facilitate assessment and cleanup of the Medical City project, the Massachusetts Department of Environmental Protection (DEP) offered technical assistance and provided accelerated timeframes for reviews/approvals of reports, permits, proposals, and risk reduction measures. DEP also assigned a Waste Site Cleanup project manager to the site, and participated in regular meetings to expedite the process. In its agreement with the WRA, the secretary of the Executive Office of Environmental Affairs wrote:

> I envision a review process that allows certain activities to proceed while the project is undergoing a full environmental review. The flexibility afforded by this modified process should prove to be more accommodating for the level of complexity associated with the state regulatory process; however, the modified review will not compromise the Environmental Impact Report review process objectives.

Artist's rendering of new Medical City facility along Worcester Center Boulevard.

With financing and public approval lined up, site improvement, environmental assessment, and remediation began to take place. Officials soon realized that transforming this patchwork of urban lots into a cohesive, developable property would be no easy task. Some of the infrastructure challenges proved to be especially daunting. A set of railroad tracks that traversed the site had to be moved; one of the city's main sewer lines had to be relocated; and 19 structures needed to be demolished. Dozens of underground storage tanks were discovered and needed to be removed; contamination included polychlorinated biphenyls (PCBs), total petroleum hydrocarbons, and metals. Where WRA could identify previous property owners, these parties were pursued and remediation costs were deducted from the price of acquiring their site.

Physical site preparation activities by the WRA included hazardous materials remediation, demolition and asbestos removal, relocation of rail lines, and site grading. All these activities were carefully coordinated to maximize and expedite the hazardous materials cleanup process. Another task involved relocating the Mill Brook sewer, a combined sewer that carried both stormwater and sewage. In the process of moving the line, the WRA decided to separate the two systems, thus benefitting downstream water quality by reducing sewage overflow during heavy rain storms. The relocation of the Providence and Worcester Railroad and site grading provided additional opportunities for cleanup.

Medical City has been classified by the DEP as a Tier IA (highest priority) hazardous materials site. The Tier IA designation was based on a number of factors, including: the extensive variety of former industrial/commercial uses, the quantity and complexity of contamination, the multiple exposure pathways in a downtown area, and the high public visibility of the project. The site required both groundwater and soil remediation, and the total quantity of soil treated or disposed exceeded 20,000 tons.

By fall 1996, all buildings on the site were demolished, soils had been remediated, and final groundwater remediation was in progress. The property is scheduled to be conveyed to the Fallon Foundation for $6.4 million, at which time DEP plans to issue Fallon a Covenant-Not-to-Sue. One final note — the Fallon Foundation in 1996 was acquired by OrNda Healthcorp, a for-profit company that is the nation's third largest healthcare provider. To handle the acquisition, the Medical City complex was expanded to include more office and parking space. According to WRA officials, the involvement of OrNda has increased the property tax revenues anticipated for the project.

Regulatory Framework

The 1992 amendments to the Massachusetts state hazardous waste management law (Chapter 21E of the Massachusetts General Laws) have encouraged faster assessment, cleanup, and redevelopment of contaminated sites. New rules for reporting, assessing, and cleaning up releases of oil and hazardous materials were codified in a completely revamped Massachusetts Contingency Plan (MCP), which took effect in October 1993. For non-priority sites, DEP no longer directly oversees site assessment and cleanup, but rather relies on private environmental engineers licensed by an independent state board, known as "Licensed Site Professionals" or "LSPs," to evaluate site conditions and oversee response actions. (DEP, however, does maintain oversight of Tier IA sites, such as Medical City.) For non-priority sites, DEP audits the results at 20 percent of all sites each year in order to ensure adherence to state cleanup standards and codes of conduct. According to the WRA's Dave Dunham, the new rules have streamlined waste cleanup procedures and encouraged greater site redevelopment. "The new Massachusetts laws have allowed us to go in with release abatement measures," he says. "Under the old law, there was too much assessment and too little remediation. Over 1,000 sites were on the state list, but very few came off."

Some of the main elements of the new MCP include: clear notification thresholds that screen out problems not likely to pose significant risks to human health or the environment, risk reduction opportunities and incentives for cleaning up small problems quickly, performance standards that allow the level of investigation to be set by the nature of the problem, generic cleanup standards for the most common contaminants, consideration of future land use at the site, clear endpoints to the process (known as Response Action Outcomes), and clarifications on liability for secured lenders and fiduciaries.

Financing

The state and WRA estimated a $42 million budget for the Medical City project (see table), with costs shared by the state and the city. Public funds were used to complete site assessment and remediation, eminent domain acquisition and relocation of occupants, building demolition and asbestos cleanup, infrastructure improvements, and site grading.

Under the provisions of Chapter 121B of the Massachusetts General Laws, public financing was bonded through the City of Worcester. The city borrowed $40 million to cover the $42-million project; over 20 years, $30.2 million in long-term bond interest will accrue. Minus the $6.4 million property price to be paid by Fallon, net project costs are $65.8 million. These costs will be divided between the city and the state, totaling $32.9 million for each. WRA officials were surprised to see budget savings in two categories: hazardous materials remediation (46 percent savings) and demolition/asbestos removal (29 percent savings). All other areas of the budget were exceeded to some degree, as illustrated in the table below.

"The biggest misnomer is that contamination carries the most influence in deciding whether to proceed with a brownfield project," says the WRA's Dave Dunham. "While it is true that the knowledge (or lack thereof) of subsurface conditions with respect to contamination most likely carries the greatest uncertainty in approaching a project, the original Medical City budget for hazardous materials and demolition/asbestos removal was 27 percent of the budget. The actual figure, in the end, will be 13 percent. So for Medical City, the greatest risk turned out to be property acquisition and relocation (nearly half the budget), despite the complexity of environmental cleanup at the site."

Medical City illustrates another interesting point: required demolition and asbestos removal activities actually created opportunities for *cost savings*. As part of site preparation activities, 19 derelict buildings were demolished in downtown Worcester. The WRA had required, as part of the permitting and contracting process, that at least 90 percent of the demolition waste be recycled. The recycling rate, in fact, reached an impressive 95 percent, thus creating a huge cost savings — $580,000 or 28 percent of the demolition budget.

Medical City Budget Status
June 30, 1996

Activity	EOCD Budget	Actual Spent to Date as of 6/30/96	WRA Projection	Projected Budget Variances
Property acquisition	$15,000,000	$12,085,010	$15,302,351	$-302,351
Business relocation	1,750,000	2,597,932	3,126,507	-1,376,507
Demolition and asbestos	2,000,000	1,419,980	1,419,980	580,019
Assessment and remediation	9,500,000	4,380,982	5,100,000	4,400,000
Site improvements	8,400,000	9,136,908	13,037,161	-4,637,161
Project management	1,550,000	2,070,110	2,388,440	-838,440
Contingency	2,000,000	0.00	0.00	2,000,000
Financing costs	1,800,000	1,625,559	1,625,559	174,440
Total Costs	42,000,000	33,316,484	42,000,000	0.00

SOURCE: Worcester Redevelopment Authority

Impacts

Once completed, Medical City will employ upwards of 3,000 people and is expected to have 1.5 million patient visits per year. During the first ten years of operation, WRA officials say, the facility's direct economic impact (direct spending) is expected to be $875 million. This will lead to an additional $1 billion in indirect economic benefits, for a total economic impact of almost $1.9 billion (the WRA estimates creation of 3,975 new state-wide jobs, with a total payroll of $765.1 million). Reports issued by WRA indicate that much of the economic benefit — including net gains in property taxes, water and sewer revenues, and parking fees — will be captured by the local Worcester area. The infusion of new spending, jobs, and visitors to the city also will have substantial indirect impacts on the value of surrounding properties, which should raise the assessed valuation base of the city as a whole.

The direct and indirect project benefits to Massachusetts are expected to produce a total of $5.8 million in sales taxes and $29 million in income taxes (for a total of $35.5 million additional state tax revenues) during the three-year construction phase and the first ten years of operation. When compared with the project's $32.9 million total cost to the state (for its 50 percent share of revenue bond retirement), there is a net revenue gain over the first ten years of $2.6 million for the state. The table below illustrates total fiscal impacts for the three-year construction period (1993-1996) and first ten years of operation.

Cumulative Economic and Fiscal Impacts of Medical City

Category of Impact	Massachusetts (in millions of 1992 dollars)	Worcester (in millions of 1992 dollars)
Direct Economic Impact	$875.0	$875.0
Total Direct and Indirect Economic Impact	$1,920.7	$1,698.3
Total Impact on Wages	$765.1	$731.6
Taxes Generated	$35.5	$11.9
Number of Additional Jobs Created	3,975	3,878

SOURCE: Bureau of Economic Analysis, RIMS II Model for the Massachusetts and Worcester County, and RKG Associates, Inc.

The Medical City project already has resulted in many other beneficial impacts. It provided for cleanup of a 24-acre hazardous materials site, the separation of the combined sewer in the downtown area, asbestos removal during demolition, recycling of 95 percent of the demolition waste, and redevelopment in an urban area as opposed to a rural "greenfield" setting. "We also made significant roadway and railway improvements, and formed a centralized downtown area that can support a commuter rail and other mass transit systems," adds the WRA's Dunham. The success of Medical City has triggered a renewed investment confidence, a revitalized downtown, high-quality jobs offering excellent career prospects, and a stable high-growth economic base.

The WRA's Dunham emphasizes the importance of choosing brownfield projects that lead to further development, so that a ripple effect of economic revitalization may occur. "You can't address one isolated brownfield and expect it to survive alone," he says. The Medical City project, in conjunction with other downtown redevelopment initiatives, has created a domino effect of economic growth in Worcester in the past five years.

The WRA, moreover, has served as a pilot for the creation of regional brownfield redevelopment authorities in Massachusetts. Because the WRA so successfully handled the myriad issues and problems associated with Medical City project, the state in 1995 passed legislation creating a regional body — the Central Massachusetts Economic Development Authority (CMEDA) — to pursue brownfield initiatives.

According to city literature, the Worcester-based CMEDA "will afford member communities an opportunity to invest in existing underutilized commercial/industrial properties, regardless of whether the properties are located within their municipal boundaries, as an alternative to...development in greenfield sites. Participating municipalities will share in real estate tax revenues produced by CMEDA's redeveloped properties. Furthermore, the authority will [have the power to] exempt the buyer from liability for past contamination. CMEDA has already been hailed by state and environmental regulatory agencies as a brownfield redevelopment model for other states and municipalities."

In 1995, the U.S. Environmental Protection Agency (EPA) awarded CMEDA a $200,000 Brownfields Pilot grant, which will be used between 1996 and 1998 to establish the authority's procedures, create a public participation model, explore financing options, prepare a manual outlining CMEDA processes, and redevelop three distinct brownfield sites.

Lessons Learned

According to participants involved with this project, development of Medical City was facilitated by the following:

Strong Cooperation Between State Agencies, Local Government, and Community Groups

Many brownfield projects are burdened by high assessment/remediation costs and by long, drawn-out time frames. One of the primary goals of the WRA, working closely with state officials and community groups, has been to slash these typical costs and shorten time frames.

In 1993, Medical City was designated a "Major and Complicated Project" by the Massachusetts's Secretary of Environmental Affairs. Under this designation, the state provided accelerated time frames for permit reviews and approvals, assigned a project manager to the site, and participated in regular meetings to expedite the redevelopment process. "What could have taken us seven years to complete was finished in just over two years," says the WRA's Dave Dunham. "The project included at least 25 different permit approvals. If each one of those approvals took DEP the standard 30-day time frame, we would have spent over 700 days just waiting for answers — that's 2½ years in delays. Instead, the usual turn-around was about one week."

The Worcester Redevelopment Authority

Establishment of the Worcester Redevelopment Authority (WRA) was critical in terms of providing the institutional framework necessary to acquire properties, coordinate remediation, and facilitate the site's redevelopment. In the case of Medical City, the WRA acted as a sort of "brownfield broker," purchasing the various properties, relocating previous owners, orchestrating site assessment and cleanup, and then handing the "clean site" over to the Fallon Foundation. The WRA cannot issue liability releases or Covenants-Not-to-Sue, but it works closely with the state DEP which does have such authority.

Amendments to Massachusetts Hazardous Waste Law

The Medical City project, says Dorothy Murray with the Massachusetts DEP, illustrates how the department has "changed from the old command-and-control strategy to a more customer service-oriented approach. The 1993 Massachusetts Contingency Plan (MCP) allowed the DEP to be more flexible, creative, and expeditious in its oversight of Medical City, thereby accelerating assessment/cleanup and reducing project costs."

Focus on Remediation Rather Than Assessment

Whenever possible, WRA officials say, one should avoid over-assessing a site before conducting remediation. Instead, an aggressive remediation program should be launched where assessment and remediation take place concurrently. For example, after initial borings in the Medical City project, many of the underground storage tank (UST) removals were performed first by removing the UST and then assessing whether contamination of soil or groundwater had occurred. Following an immediate assessment (with a portable kit), the contamination was removed quickly and efficiently. "With a brownfield redevelopment," suggests WRA's Dunham, "don't waste time and money on too much early assessment. Remediation is the final objective."

Rough Grading of the Site, Which Allowed Discovery of Site Contamination

Most brownfield sites have a "background contamination" that can be discerned through examining site history. Provided that the contaminants are non-migratory and non-leachable (e.g., coal ash and some metals), the public health exposure pathways can be eliminated by capping the site with impervious surfaces, such as buildings, asphalt, and clean fill. For the Medical City project, the WRA employed such an approach. First, officials "rough graded" the site to discover all foreseeable contamination at the outset; second, the redeveloper capped the site with final grades and structures.

Innovative Technological Approaches

Throughout assessment and remediation activities, the WRA attempted to defray costs by using innovative technological approaches. For example, Ground Penetrating Radar was employed to identify potential locations of USTs; soil vapor extraction was used to remediate soils contaminated with chlorinated solvents; a sparge/vent system, in tandem with traditional groundwater recovery, was used for groundwater remediation; and a vapor barrier/underslab venting system will protect the hospital from any potential air contamination from groundwater. These technological approaches produced significant costs savings in the remediation portions of the project.

Construction Activities that Addressed Environmental Contamination

The WRA successfully used construction operations as a way to assess and remediate environmental contamination that might not have been discovered until later. Much of the site's assessment and remediation occurred during relocation of the railroad, roadways, and major utilities, and also during demolition and site grading. According to the WRA, this approach produced significant cost-savings and ensured a thorough cleanup of the site.

Contacts

Dave Dunham
Worcester Redevelopment Authority
(508) 799-5500

Dorothy Murray
Central Regional Office
Massachusetts Department of Environmental Protection
(508) 792-7653 ext. 3834

THE LAWRENCE GATEWAY PROJECT
(Oxford Paper Site)
Lawrence, Massachusetts

Key Players

- City of Lawrence — local government; oversight agency.
- GenCorp Polymer Products — neighboring business; financed significant portion of cleanup at Oxford facility.
- Massachusetts Highway Department — state agency conducting road improvements.
- Lawrence Into Action — local community group.

Background and Nature of the Problem

Since the 1850s, Lawrence, Massachusetts, has been a magnet for workers immigrating to the U.S. in search of work. Recognized as one of the first planned industrial cities in America, Lawrence became a leading powerhouse in the production of textiles and paper during the Industrial Revolution. The city is famous for its mills, which were built along a maze of canals and underground water power systems fed by the Spicket and Merrimack Rivers. In 1912, Lawrence secured its place on the map with the famous Bread and Roses strike, an event that forever changed child and general labor practices in this country.

Like many industrial towns, however, Lawrence has witnessed a steady decline in manufacturing in recent years. While Massachusetts was riding the economic wave of the 1980s, the City of Lawrence lost nearly 7,000 jobs and became the 23rd poorest city in the nation, with the lowest per-capita income in the state. Job losses, coupled with an increase in population, by 1995 had given rise to a 10.3 percent unemployment rate, the highest in Massachusetts. Since the late 1980s, Lawrence's tax base has been cut in half. Many of its largest mills have sat idle for decades, a bitter reminder of this city's once thriving economy. A walk through downtown reveals scores of empty lots, boarded up buildings and tenements, many of which have reverted to city ownership. "The image of Lawrence is basically that we have a lot of larceny and car thefts," says Kathy

Hersh, co-chair of the citizen group, Lawrence Into Action, "but that's not what this town is about."

Redefining Lawrence's image has become a priority for local planners and concerned residents. Most recognize that the city's historic mills, now a blighting influence on the community, represent the key to future growth. Reusing the sites would stimulate job creation and boost the city's depressed tax base. In addition, Lawrence has many attributes that make it an attractive place for growth — direct access to two major highways, an industrial/commuter rail line, a nearby municipal airport, and most importantly, a rich cultural and architectural history that defines the city's character. Despite these qualities, many of the old mills remain empty or under-utilized because of widespread fear about environmental contamination. With a few exceptions, Massachusetts law holds that purchasers of brownfield sites enter into the chain of liability, thus assuming responsibility for any pollution that might be present.

The most visible brownfield in Lawrence is the sprawling Oxford Paper site on Canal Street, located at the gateway to the historic, industrial part of town. For over 135 years, the Oxford site produced high-quality paper, employing 700 people at its peak during the 1950s. National Geographic bought the company in 1935 in order to ensure a constant supply of Oxford's vaunted paper for its publication needs. Starting in the 1960s, however, ownership of the property changed hands several times, and by 1974 the plant was shut down altogether. The site was dispersed among five partners of a local real estate company, who, in turn, sold off portions of the property to area businesses. The partners were not able to unload Oxford's larger manufacturing buildings, however, and by the early 1980s, these structures — spanning just over three acres — reverted to the city through tax delinquency.

Lawrence, therefore, became saddled with a real estate nightmare. The Oxford site routinely was plundered by scavengers, arsonists, and illegal dumpers. Trespassers broke into the buildings to strip transformers and reclaim the salvageable parts, often releasing polychlorinated biphenyls (PCBs) into the ground. Eventually the city was forced to fence off the property. Several large fires swept through the buildings in the 1970s and 1980s, leaving charred, unstable structures in their wake. "You can look into the buildings and clearly see asbestos," says Christine Mizioch, environmental project manager for the Massachusetts Highway Department. "When the wind blows, the asbestos is stirred up —

something that is definitely not positive for the surrounding neighborhood, especially since there's a hospital nearby."

In 1986, the Massachusetts Department of Environmental Protection (DEP) identified the site as being marginally contaminated but posing no apparent imminent danger to public health or the environment. It took another ten years, until summer of 1996, for DEP to formally classify the site as a Tier IB property under the state's Superfund program. Tier IB sites are less contaminated than Tier IA sites (which are the most serious, requiring direct DEP oversight), but more contaminated than Tier IC or II sites.

One neighbor receiving Oxford's contamination is GenCorp Polymer Products (GenCorp), an old rubber manufacturer that shut down its Lawrence operations in 1981. GenCorp has vacated most of its 22 buildings, but a small staff remains to oversee environmental compliance issues. Unlike Oxford, GenCorp's eight-acre site has not fallen into disrepair (a round-the-clock security team guards the property). However, like Oxford, the site is classified as Tier 1B. To complicate its environmental situation, GenCorp's property is linked directly to the Oxford site because of a shared "raceway" between the two companies. The raceway is an old underground spillway for industrial wastewater that flows back and forth between the two plants, discharging ultimately into the Spicket River. Because of the raceway, there is a constant commingling of materials and contaminants from the two sites that makes separating each company's contribution virtually impossible. GenCorp has assumed responsibility for PCBs discovered in the raceway, but for many other contaminants, liability is less clear.

In the early 1990s, the City of Lawrence faced mounting pressure from local residents to clean up the Oxford site, but officials were shackled because of non-existent municipal funds. Unable to act, they began seeking viable potentially responsible parties (PRPs) that could be held liable for site cleanup. They looked no further than GenCorp — whose raceway connection with Oxford, and whose deep-pocket corporate status, made the company an attractive target. In retrospect, city officials admit that trying to label GenCorp a PRP at the Oxford site was a mistake — "just plain incorrect," says a former city employee. The city's move jeopardized relations with GenCorp, and it would take several years before the dust settled and a viable new partnership emerged.

Meeting the Challenge

In 1994, Lawrence officials decided to use a portion of their annual Community Development Block Grant (CDBG) funds to hire a full-time staff person — Kevin Geaney — who would oversee the Oxford Paper site. This was a critical step in breaking the impasse that had stymied cleanup and redevelopment initiatives in years past. "Hiring Kevin was the catalyst," says Kathy Hersh with Lawrence Into Action. "Now there was one person in City Hall whose one responsibility was [dealing with] this project."

Geaney immediately took a different tack than his predecessors. "I advised them that their approach of searching for PRPs wasn't financially or legally achievable," says Geaney. "The city was, in fact, the liable and responsible party and had to begin looking at ways to deal with its responsibility." Geaney was instrumental in forging a cooperative partnership between the city and GenCorp. Due to the complexity of the Oxford site and Lawrence's limited finances, the city requested that GenCorp act in an "advisory capacity" for environmental, technical, and reuse issues at Oxford's site. GenCorp agreed to this, but the company also decided to partially finance assessment and cleanup activities at its neighboring Oxford site — to the tune of over $800,000. "We can't do the city's work," explains Bob Devaney, director of environmental engineering for GenCorp's Lawrence office. "So they do it, and we reimburse them."

"GenCorp sees that it's in its best interest to participate in the cleanup of Oxford's site, ensure that all buildings are demolished, and participate in redevelopment initiatives," says the city's Geaney. "Many companies have chosen to encapsulate and fence off their properties, but GenCorp made a conscious decision to act responsibly. It's extraordinary [when] a company [does] this."

As Geaney contemplated reuse options for the Oxford site, he began examining local planning efforts underway in the immediate area. "We looked at the Oxford site and other projects nearby and tried to find ways to integrate them all in an effort to lessen the city's overall liability burden," says Geaney. He learned that city officials were planning to replace the nearby historic Canal Street Bridge and add a new traffic interchange — all within the vicinity of the Oxford Paper plant. Could these two projects be linked, Geaney wondered, essentially forming a new "gateway" to the city? If the main traffic artery were shifted 100 feet to the north, it would pass right through the Oxford site. This would enable the cash-strapped city to draw on Massachusetts Highway Department funds to pay for demolition and site improvements at the Oxford property — an innovative financing solution that would tackle two objectives at once.

Geaney sat down with GenCorp representatives and hammered out a plan. They worked closely with Lawrence Into Action, the local community organization. This 30-member group brought together local business people, government representatives, neighborhood groups, historical preservationists, and environmental interests. "There's a commitment in this area that goes beyond the norm," says Lawrence Into Action's Hersh. "It's more than just about starting a group. You have to believe in your heart that your mission is essential. In our case, the circumstances were just right, all the pieces came together at exactly the right time." What emerged from this community visioning process was the blueprint for the Lawrence Gateway Project — a conceptual plan to revitalize the city by restoring its historic entrance at the Canal Street Bridge near the Oxford Paper plant.

Lawrence's Oxford Paper plant, Marston Street looking west.

Turning this vision into a reality, however, would be no easy job. Among the most challenging aspects were coordinating the multiple permitting and oversight issues for the bridge enhancement project and cleanup at both the Oxford and GenCorp sites — tasks complicated by the virtual army of federal, state, and local decision makers involved. The federal agencies working on the project include the U.S. Army Corps of Engineers, U.S. Advisory Council on Historic Preservation (the Oxford buildings are listed on the National Register of Historic Places), and U.S. Environmental Protection Agency (EPA) — three agencies whose missions do not always jibe with one another. This group was augmented by a team of state agencies, including the Massachusetts DEP, the Massachusetts Highway Department, the Executive Office of Environmental Affairs, and the Massachusetts Historical Commission. Several city offices also are involved. To coordinate these many voices, two inter-agency task forces were formed to handle technical and administrative issues. "Our goal was to bring the various decision makers together, to find opportunities to advance permitting issues, and to close the gaps between each different agency's jurisdictions," says the city's Geaney. Many believe that these task forces, by expediting permit approvals and streamlining decisionmaking, have been the key to the Lawrence Gateway Project's success to date.

Another important aspect of the Lawrence Gateway Project was strong involvement by legislators. Congressman Marty Meehan (D-MA) took an active role in encouraging public/private partnerships and securing funds. "Our goal is to make connections happen," says Bob LaRochelle, director of economic development for Rep. Meehan. "We [believed] that the City of Lawrence didn't have the capacity to apply for federal grants or, once obtained, to implement them. So we asked GenCorp and the Merrimack College's Urban Institute to work with the city and help write the necessary proposals. One $25,000 grant from the Massachusetts Land Bank was a direct request from Marty. His involvement with the Lawrence Gateway Project has been on every level — if he has to pick up the phone to get involved himself, he doesn't hesitate." Rep. Meehan also was instrumental in securing $500,000 in roadway enhancement funds for the project through the Intermodal Surface Transportation Efficiency Act (ISTEA). Meehan's success in securing public funds, says Bob LaRochelle, hinged on inviting top government officials to tour Lawrence — including Housing and Urban Development (HUD) Secretary Henry Cisneros and various EPA personnel. "We impressed upon them the city's many problems," says LaRochelle, "but, more importantly, we emphasized that this is an active community interested in pulling itself up by its bootstraps, which makes officials much more willing to commit public money."

Aerial view of Oxford Paper plant.

In fall 1995, the city hired a contractor to complete site assessment work at the Oxford property. Because most of the buildings are structurally unstable, workers could not enter them to conduct the assessments. "A lot of the work was done on inference, talking to prior employees and people connected with the site," says Christine Mizioch with the Massachusetts Highway Department. "We just tried to get a best estimate of site conditions." Preliminary results indicated the presence of asbestos, lead paint, and PCBs. In spring 1997, the city will submit a remediation plan and final demolition specifications to the Massachusetts DEP. Department officials expect that, once both plans are reviewed, demolition at the Oxford site can begin, probably by summer 1997. When the buildings are demolished, secondary assessment of soil conditions underneath the old structures will take place.

Plans call for leaving the existing, historical bridge in place and transforming it into a pedestrian crossing of the Spicket River, complete with ornamental lighting. A new arched bridge will be built to handle automotive traffic. Some of the Oxford site will be used for access roadways, but, on the remaining open space, city officials plan to create a park. In spring 1998, officials expect to begin building the new road and bridge that will form the backbone of the Lawrence Gateway Project.

During the demolition and construction phases, the city will transfer to the state custody of, but not liability for, the Oxford property. After improvements are complete, and when the site is fully graded and seeded, custody of the Gateway area will revert back to the city. DEP may allow certain contaminants to be left on site, provided that appropriate protections (e.g., a layer of top soil) are put in place to reduce human exposure to contaminants. If this is the case, DEP will require that an "activity and use limitation" restriction be placed on the property, in accordance with the Massachusetts Contingency Plan (MCP), so that inappropriate uses, such as residential housing, never occur there in the future. The restriction will be recorded at the local registry of deeds and will stay with the property's title of ownership.

All the buildings on the Oxford Site are on the National Register of Historic Places. To move forward with the project, the State Highway Department had to enter into a Memorandum of Understanding with the Massachusetts Historical Commission, the Federal Highway Administration, and the U.S. Advisory Council on Historic Preservation. "We have to provide documentation of buildings before demolition for the National Archives," says the Highway Department's Mizioch.

While demolition at the Oxford site is pending, GenCorp already has demolished over half its own buildings and remediated 30 percent of the property. The company has spent more than $40 million on site assessment, remediation, and demolition activities; an additional $33 million will be spent before the project is complete. GenCorp plans to leave only one 100,000 square-foot structure on the site. The cleared areas will provide green space and some much-needed public parking. According to GenCorp's Bob Devaney, "Business owners in the area have indicated that public parking is absolutely critical in terms of advancing economic revitalization. Here is an example where corporate interest and community interest clearly came together."

Regulatory Framework

The regulatory mechanism used to assess and remediate the Oxford and GenCorp sites is the Massachusetts 21E program, the state Superfund law. Procedures for the 21E program are outlined in the Massachusetts Contingency Plan — a series of rules that enable regulators to categorize, determine oversight procedures, and set standards for the cleanup of sites.

Liability provisions under the Massachusetts 21E program are strict, joint, and several. Potentially responsible parties (PRPs) include current owners, past owners (where it can be proven they are responsible for contamination), and generators and transporters of site contaminants. Lenders that own sites prior to foreclosure, or which hold interest in a site, may be exempted from liability provided they did not cause or help cause contamination, and provided they take measures necessary to eliminate contaminant exposure. The same is applicable to local governments, as long as their foreclosed sites are due to tax delinquency.

Federal statutes that apply to the Lawrence Gateway Project include: the Resource Conservation and Recovery Act (RCRA), the Toxic Substances Control Act (TSCA), the Comprehensive Environmental Response, Compensation, and Liability Act (CERCLA), and the Clean Water Act (CWA).

Financing

The city anticipates that total costs for the Lawrence Gateway Project will be upwards of $8 million — with remediation and demolition totaling $3.5 million and bridge/road construction totaling $4.5 million. With the exception of GenCorp's $800,000 contribution for assessment and cleanup at Oxford's site, the project is being funded solely by public-sector entities. According to the city's Kevin Geaney, however, this may change soon. "In the near future," Geaney says, "we expect several banks to contribute in the neighborhood of $5,000-$10,000 each towards the Gateway Project. The banks benefit because [the initiative] will add value to properties throughout the area."

Expenditures at the Oxford site to date have exceeded $1.6 million. The City of Lawrence has dedicated over $575,000 of its Community Development Block Grant (CDBG) funds since 1994; the Massachusetts Land Bank Grant Fund, an independent state development agency, awarded Lawrence a $25,000 grant; and EPA in 1995 provided the city a $200,000 grant under its Brownfields Pilot Site Program.

The bulk of funding for the Lawrence Gateway Project was secured through the Massachusetts Highway Department, which dedicated $4.5 million for demolition and remediation at the Oxford site, as well as construction of the new Canal Street bridge and a traffic interchange. The Federal Highway Administration contributes 80 percent of this money, the state provides the remaining 20 percent. The city also secured $500,000 in enhancement funds under the federal Intermodal Surface Transportation and Efficiency Act (ISTEA). ISTEA money cannot be used for any demolition or construction activities; instead, it will fund Gateway corridor studies for establishment of a historic, scenic parkway.

The City of Lawrence recently was designated by the state as both an Economic Opportunity Area and an Economic Target Area. These designations enable the city to offer tax incentives for new businesses that locate there, as well as to directly fund job-training programs for employees. These programs, coupled with new laws offering liability protection for certain parties, serve to encourage the reuse of older, industrial properties in the city.

For its part, GenCorp has spent over $40 million to date on cleanup at its site. Officials anticipate spending at least $33 million more before completion.

Impacts

According to city officials, the Lawrence Gateway Project has triggered a domino effect of revitalization in Lawrence's historic industrial district. Encouraged by redevelopment at the Oxford Paper site, public and private investors already have committed over $160 million for improvements in the surrounding area.

A new public/private corporation, called the Lawrence Initiative, has been established to effectively manage and coordinate financing for brownfield projects. Although the existing community organization, Lawrence In Action, currently has some public representation in its ranks, the Lawrence Initiative will have a much stronger public component. The group will not have official implementation powers, but will instead provide a forum for consensus development. It will receive both public and private funds, and will enjoy a 501(c)(3) tax-deductible status. "When you take these issues to the next level and the important issues of consensus arrive, you need a public/private corporation to handle them. The new Lawrence

Initiative will have a broader perspective and participation, starting in the Gateway Project area and then expanding to other parts of the city," says the city's Geaney.

Lessons Learned

According to participants involved with this project, the Lawrence Gateway Project was facilitated by the following:

Strong Public/Private Partnership

The Lawrence Gateway Project benefitted from an intensely strong public/private partnership, which formed in 1994 between the City of Lawrence, GenCorp, and the community group Lawrence Into Action. "We recognized that the interests of the City of Lawrence and GenCorp are parallel," says Bob Devaney of GenCorp. "As the city does better, GenCorp does better. It's one of these classic situations where the pie is very big and everyone gets a slice."

As plans for the Gateway Project coalesced, the partnership grew to include a wide range of state and federal agencies, local businesses, legislators, and residents. The inter-agency task forces (comprised of local, state, and federal representatives) were critical in terms of streamlining decision making and coordinating the multiple regulatory issues connected with the project. "They decided that they all had to work together, and it's been incredibly successful," says Devaney. "If it wasn't for [the task forces], we wouldn't have been able to move forward." Kevin Geaney adds that "Governor Weld's office, and particularly the Executive Office of Environmental Affairs, is very pro-business. They've been able to mesh the goals and objectives of business and environmental remediation. There's a climate that allows cities to get in the trenches and pursue projects."

GenCorp's Devaney points out that the link with legislators also has been essential. "None of these projects exists in a vacuum. The Gateway process was the product of a continuous communication effort at the local, state, and federal level," he says. There easily could have been political wrangling because Lawrence's Mayor Mary Claire Kennedy is a Republican, while the district Congressman, Marty Meehan, is a Democrat. "But the whole notion that you can't work together because you're of different political parties is something we don't buy here," says Bob LaRochelle, Rep. Meehan's director of economic development. "The bottom line is that we need to address these problems across political parties by involving the public sector and neighborhoods. Federal and state agencies are more willing to invest in communities that do that." GenCorp's Devaney agrees, "There are a lot of reasons why things can't work; you've got to look for ways to *make* them work."

Incorporating Oxford Site Reuse into the City's Broader "Vision" for Growth

One of the most important aspects of the Gateway Project was strong community vision. "We looked at the other programs going on in Lawrence to see if they matched our goals — and, in fact, there were many overlaps," says the city's Geaney. "We were suggesting a comprehensive, holistic approach to brownfields, looking for connections with other programs and initiatives. The result was a corridor approach. We saw that you can mold brownfield initiatives so that they mesh with other transportation and economic development initiatives."

Kathy Hersh of Lawrence Into Action agrees. "Every level of government, every private-sector partner was involved and focused and had a vision," she notes. The Lawrence Gateway "visioning" process was launched in 1994 with a series of brainstorming sessions intended to determine the project's scope. "I really tried to get the group to expand the focus to include Essex Street [two blocks away]," says Hersh, "but they strongly felt that we should retain our focus on Canal Street." In retrospect, Hersh believes that her colleagues were right — that it's more effective to start small and achieve concrete results before tackling a wider area. In fact, the city is confident that triggering redevelopment in this small area, the city's gateway, will spur development throughout the rest of Lawrence.

Lawrence's "visioning" process is constantly expanding and bringing in new players. In 1994, the city unsuccessfully applied to be a HUD-designated Enterprise Community. "We weren't selected," says Bob LaRochelle in Congressman Meehan's office, "but the application process was very helpful. People who had never talked to each other were now working together towards a common goal." The important thing, says GenCorp's Bob Devaney, is to "always keep an open mind. New issues will come up as the process evolves. What's important is to remain flexible and adjust your tactics."

Strong Leadership at the Local Level

"In order for these initiatives to go forward — to get disparate parties to whistle the same tune — there has to be some coordination," says the city's Geaney, "and that coordination definitely falls on the local community. People who've worked in the trenches at the local level are just better equipped than people at higher levels to oversee these kinds of projects." In this case, the local point person for the City of Lawrence has been Kevin Geaney. "He pretty much holds everything together, makes sure everyone's needs are met," says the Massachusetts Highway Department's Mizioch. "The city really has pushed the coordinated effort [on this project], given us lots of information and guidance. Sometimes we can't get cooperation at the local level, but in this case, working together has helped us stay on the critical path."

Geaney points out that because state and federal officials involved with the project focus only on their particular task, they don't necessarily grasp the entire picture. "When I talk to EPA people," Geaney states, "they don't want to hear about the fact that we received Highway Department funds for this project — it would create an enormous accounting problem for them, not to mention the philosophical nightmare" of working with an agency so different from their own.

Community Involvement From the Outset

"One of the steps that gets overlooked too often is the consensus development process," says the city's Geaney. Lawrence's community group, Lawrence Into Action, actively supported the hiring of a consultant, encouraged the city to coordinate the road/bridge project with the Oxford site cleanup, encouraged a corridor study that evolved into an ISTEA grant, and made the case for the EPA brownfield grant. All stakeholders agree that involvement of Lawrence Into Action has been critical to the project's success.

Corporate Leadership

The Lawrence Gateway Project illustrates that public- and private-sector objectives often can jibe. In this case, both the city and GenCorp sought to promote environmental cleanup and economic growth in the area. "GenCorp is a very corporate-responsible operation with a commitment to its community," says Bob LaRochelle from Congressman Meehan's office. While GenCorp has been praised widely for its support of Oxford, company officials maintain that cleaning up the site simply makes good business sense. "Environmental problems at the Oxford site slow us down," says GenCorp's

Devaney. "Remediating that site helps to speed up our own cleanup process."

Drawing on the Particular Strengths and Attributes of Lawrence

In launching the Lawrence Gateway Project, officials tapped into two of the city's key attributes: its strong industrial legacy and its proximity to the Spicket and Merrimack Rivers. By virtue of its location, the Gateway Project celebrates the older, historic section of town, essentially reconnecting residents with their roots. The project also includes an open space and "green corridor" component, which will make the rivers more accessible for public enjoyment and recreation.

Lawrence officials recently noted, "Cities with abandoned industrial sites located in historical districts, such as Lawrence, and many other cities located in the eastern half of the United States, have an opportunity to leverage relatively small investments to induce much larger investments by developers and other industrial or commercial businesses. This is particularly the case where, as with the Lawrence Gateway District, various types of contamination specific to industrial sites are located within areas that include waterways, historical buildings, and other amenities that have inherent value due to their quaintness and aura of permanence."

Contacts

Bob Luongo
Economic Development Coordinator
Mayor's Office
City of Lawrence
(508) 794-5858

Bob Devaney
Director, Environmental Engineering
GenCorp in Lawrence
(508) 683-7123

CAROL CABLE PLANT
(Display World)
Warren, Rhode Island

Key Players

- Mount Hope Enterprise Zone — local council that oversees this state-designated opportunity area.
- Rhode Island Department of Environmental Management — state environmental agency.
- Rhode Island Economic Development Corporation — state development agency.
- Rhode Island Department of Transportation — state transportation agency.
- General Cable Company (Carol Cable) — property seller.
- Display World, Inc. — purchaser.

Background and Nature of Problem

Warren, Rhode Island, is a small town, population 11,000, located ten miles southeast of Providence along the Narragansett Bay. It historically has been a blue-collar town, supported by the bustling mills nearby. One prominent mill, the Carol Cable plant, is a three-story brick behemoth that was built in 1899. The 240,000-square-foot facility produced textiles until the late 1960s, employing nearly 300 workers at its peak. From 1968 to 1990, automotive wire, car battery terminals, and cable products were manufactured there. Then, in 1990, operations ceased and the Rhode Island Department of Environmental Management (DEM) stepped in, ordering General Cable Company, the parent company of Carol Cable, to conduct environmental assessments.

Investigations at the site revealed petroleum contamination from oil spills and lead contamination from the manufacture of car battery terminals. General Cable agreed to voluntarily remediate the site under DEM supervision. By 1994, the major petroleum and lead hotspots had been excavated from soils at the site, but residual lead contamination remained along the banks of an old cooling water pond. "The state's water cleanup standards were incredibly high —

almost unattainable," notes Alan Crisman, executive director of the Mount Hope Enterprise Zone, a state-designated economic opportunity area in which the Carol Cable plant is located. "General Cable and DEM couldn't agree on what an effective remediation plan would be to achieve those standards." As a result, the water quality issues lingered and remained unresolved.

Meeting the Challenge

In fall 1995, Display World Inc., a retail display manufacturer, announced its interest in purchasing the Carol Cable plant. Display World had outgrown its present facility and was searching for a single-story, 100,000-square-foot plant in which to expand. The manufacturer employed 75 people at the time and pledged to create 50 more jobs. Display World officials concluded that Carol Cable was the ideal site (the second and third floors, they decided, could be leased out). For the deal to proceed, however, company officials needed all lingering environmental issues and liability questions resolved. To complicate matters, the purchaser — in order to secure financing — established an unprecedented turnaround time of three days in which to map out the transaction.

Alan Crisman of the Mount Hope Enterprise Zone describes how the events unfolded. "Ray Angers, president of Display World, walked into my office at 11:00 a.m. on a Monday morning and said he was interested in the property but he needed DEM clearance," Crisman says. "So I called DEM's Terry Gray and told him we needed to finish the environmental work on Carol Cable. Terry said, 'I can meet in two weeks.' I said, 'Terry, what are you doing tomorrow morning at 11:00 a.m.?'"

To DEM's credit, the group did meet the following morning. Fortunately, only three months earlier, the state legislature had passed Rhode Island's Industrial Property Remediation and Reuse Act, which included many provisions designed to encourage cleanup and redevelopment of brownfield sites like the Carol Cable plant. For example, liability relief was now available for innocent parties (e.g., Display World) that take title to contaminated properties. In addition, the law called for creation of new cleanup standards — ones that would consider use of engineering and institutional controls, instead of relying solely on removals, to meet state requirements. This change would have a profound impact at the Carol Cable site, which had been in regulatory limbo for over a year due to the lead residuals in its cooling water pond.

Carol Cable plant.

Just prior to Tuesday's meeting, DEM's water resources staff had instructed General Cable to install certain engineering controls — effectively implementing a final remedy at the site. Once this remedy was complete, the water department would support issuance of a Covenant-Not-to-Sue. There would be further complications, however. It turned out that the cooling water pond was located in a state-delineated wetland area. Normally, wetland alterations in Rhode Island trigger a complicated permitting process that can take upwards of a year to complete. Under state law, though, when a remedial action is being conducted, an exemption from the state wetland alteration permitting process may be granted. Such "exempted" projects are subject to a consistency review by the wetlands staff at DEM. Since this system of review, while less time-consuming than the formal wetlands permitting process, also can be lengthy, DEM's Division of Site Remediation made it a priority to slash the usual time frame to meet Display World's needs. "In complex and time-critical projects, my staff essentially becomes a project manager for the site," says DEM's Gray. "We literally walked the Carol Cable property through the review process with the wetland staff."

In February 1996, a Settlement Agreement was signed by DEM, Display World, and General Cable. The agreement spelled out the remedial scope of work and contained a Covenant-Not-to-Sue provision for the buyer, Display World, that would become effective when cleanup was completed.

In this case, the final remedy involved implementing a series of engineering controls for the cooling water pond. The challenge was to prevent pond sediments from migrating into the receiving waterway below. This migration had been ongoing for many years, the result of a relief pipe that had connected an underground spring to the pond, causing a constant overflow of water. DEM's goal was to stabilize the pond water and, in so doing, immobilize the contaminants. State officials ordered that the relief pipe be re-routed and the spillway level raised in order to allow only periodic overflows from the pond.

Less than a month after the Settlement Agreement was signed, at the end of February 1996, the engineering controls were in place and DEM issued Display World a letter of compliance. The Carol Cable plant became the first industrial site to proceed through Rhode Island's Voluntary Cleanup Program.

Carol Cable plant.

Regulatory Framework

Rhode Island's Voluntary Cleanup Program (VCP), in place since 1993, was revised in July 1995 by the Industrial Property Remediation and Reuse Act. The Industrial Property Remediation and Reuse Program offers liability relief to third parties and financial institutions participating in the program. Supportive tax credits were approved by the state legislature in 1996.

Regulations specifying soil cleanup standards, promulgated in August 1996, are intended to reflect the current and future land use at a site, and to conform with existing groundwater classifications. The regulations contemplate a modified Risk-Based Corrective Action (RBCA) approach to managing areas that have been impacted by a release of hazardous materials. Four basic classes of standards are outlined in the regulations:

- direct exposure criteria for industrial land use;
- direct exposure criteria for residential land use;
- leachability criteria for protection of groundwater resources used for drinking water; and
- leachability criteria for protection of groundwater resources in urban areas.

Financing

Display World planned to purchase the Carol Cable property and conduct a series of renovations. However, the firm's bank was reluctant to lend money until all remedial work had been completed — something that caught DEM officials by surprise. "Our assumption was that a [promise of a] Covenant-Not-to Sue by the state, based on a specific, negotiated scope of work for cleanup, would be sufficient for funding the project prior to completion of work," DEM said. "We believe this issue may be related to the fact that the program is very new and the financial community has not become completely aware of our efforts."

The Carol Cable property is located within the Mount Hope Enterprise Zone, a state-designated area that encompasses all of Warren and parts of nearby Bristol, Rhode Island. The state offers economic incentives to new companies that locate inside the zone. As such, Display World could take advantage of tax breaks for each new Rhode Island resident employed at the Warren site, as well as tax breaks on all renovations completed. "[The redevelopment of Carol

Cable] is a tremendous story for Rhode Island," Alan Crisman, executive director of the Mount Hope Enterprise Zone, told the *Providence Journal* in November 1995. "It's a tremendous story for the Enterprise Zone. It's an absolute home run."

In January 1996, EPA awarded Rhode Island a $200,000 Brownfield Pilot Site grant, which is being used to identify and assess several brownfield sites in the Providence area. Governor Lincoln Almond told reporters at the time, "Today's grant is great news for Rhode Island, the birthplace of the Industrial Revolution. It's time we cleaned these sites so they can again be used as centers of employment. We began that process when we welcomed Display World to a brownfield site, and this grant will help us build momentum."

Impacts

Ray Angers, president of Display World, purchased the Carol Cable property for $175,000 and then spent over $500,000 on lighting improvements and roof repairs. "It was a good deal for him and a good deal for the town. There weren't any losers on this deal," says Alan Crisman. Display World brought 75 existing jobs to the area and created approximately 50 new ones. At present, 70,000 square feet of the building's space remains vacant. "We are trying to attract a small business incubator for that space. Ultimately, the building may employ between 300-400 people," says Crisman.

Lessons Learned

According to participants involved with this project, redevelopment of the Carol Cable plant was facilitated by the following:

Rhode Island's New Brownfields Law

The 1995 Industrial Property Remediation and Reuse Act has had a significant impact on brownfield projects in Rhode Island. DEM has identified the Covenant-Not-to-Sue as the most important tool available to encourage brownfields cleanup and reuse in the state. The covenant provides much needed clarity and closure to the cleanup process — something that should encourage increased lending by banks on such projects.

In the case of the Carol Cable plant, residual contaminants at the site raised a red flag for the purchaser, Display World. "Residuals pose a problem," notes Tim O'Connor, program manager for the state remediation program, "because agency policy is subject to change and current laws may change. Levels that are acceptable today might not be tomorrow." Display World was wary of this uncertainty. Not willing to risk potential environmental liability down the road, company officials announced that, without proper releases and assurances, they would simply relocate elsewhere. Fortunately, the 1995 law had recently been enacted and Display World could obtain this necessary sign-off. "Without the brownfield legislation, there's no way this deal would have happened," says Alan Crisman with the Mount Hope Enterprise Zone. "It allowed us to take a building that was six months away from being a pile of rubble and turn it into a major employment center, as it has been for most of this century."

Adoption of Standardized Cleanup Levels

Rhode Island's new Industrial Property Remediation and Reuse Act established as law many aspects of the state Voluntary Cleanup Program that had been in place since 1993. The law codified that cleanup standards should be proportional to a property's end use. The legislature directed DEM, with formal public involvement, to develop soil cleanup standards that were "consistent with current and reasonable foreseeable future use of properties." These standards were promulgated in fall 1996.

Alan Crisman of the Mount Hope Enterprise Zone notes that the new cleanup standards were critical for the Carol Cable project to move forward. "Now you can have containment, as opposed to just removal, to meet state standards. Before, we would have had to de-water the pond at the Carol Cable site — a totally unrealistic option." DEM's Tim O'Connor agrees, "These standards will help us bypass time-consuming site-specific assessments. In the past, reporting requirements were very subjective, not numerical. The standard was eliminating 'adverse effects to human health or environment.' Now we have numerical values, and we can define a solid end point."

Strong Project Management and Inter-Agency Coordination

State officials made it a priority to move this project through the review process in an expedited fashion. "What happens normally is that General Cable would have had to apply to all the different offices independently for their permits — water, wetlands, and site remediation," says DEM's Terry Gray. "They wouldn't have been ushered through the system like this. Bottom line is: you've got to have a project manager that takes over ownership of the project and shepherds it through the individual administrative processes." In this case, DEM's Division of Site Remediation acted as the de facto project manager.

A fast turnaround on remedial activities was critical because Ray Angers, president of Display World, needed to secure financing for his proposed renovations. As DEM's Gray explains, "Display World's bank was financing rehabilitation of the building, but the bank wouldn't loan until the Covenant-Not-to-Sue had vested, and the covenant wouldn't vest until work was completed. So you can see that this really put a lot of pressure on DEM to expedite the remedial process." According to Jim Saletnik, technical assistance coordinator for the Rhode Island Economic Development Corporation, "DEM was extremely responsive. The bank was reluctant to lend because of the potential liability situation; DEM had a lot to do with getting this transaction done so quickly." Saletnik adds that cooperation between different state agencies also has been excellent under Governor Almond's administration: "This thing could not have happened if DEM and the Economic Development Corporation hadn't worked so well together."

The Rhode Island Department of Transportation (DOT) also played a key role in this project. Display World officials had insisted, at the outset, that DOT install a pedestrian-controlled stoplight on the state highway for their employees' safety. "DOT made the guarantee, found the money, and installed the light in an exceedingly short period of time," says the Mount Hope Enterprise Zone's Crisman. "Since [Display World] moved in a week before the installation was complete, the Town of Warren provided a police officer as a crossing guard for the week. Everyone had a role to play and everyone worked together superbly."

Carol Cable's Location in the Mount Hope Enterprise Zone

"The Enterprise Zone streamlined the overall permitting procedure," says Crisman. "I have to say, it really works. When I talked to DEM's Terry Grey the first time, he didn't know me from Adam." But Grey bent over backwards to push the deal through. "And I just don't think the project would have happened," Crisman explains, "without the Enterprise Zone legislation, which mandates inter-departmental coordination." Crisman also adds that the interests of the Mount Hope Enterprise Zone and the DEM dovetailed nicely, resulting in mutual benefit for both groups. "DEM was looking for a brownfield poster child," Crisman says, referring to the fact that Rhode Island's brownfield program was brand new and public officials were eager to highlight a local "success story."

Contacts

Alan Crisman
Executive Director
Mount Hope Enterprise Zone
(401) 245-4222

Terrence Gray
Director
Office of Waste Management
Rhode Island Department of Environmental Management
(401) 277-3872

Jim Saletnik
Rhode Island Economic Development Corporation
(401) 277-2601

BRYANT ELECTRIC PLANT
Bridgeport, Connecticut

Key Players

- Bridgeport Office of Planning and Economic Development — local planning agency.
- West End Community Development Corporation — local non-profit development corporation.
- Connecticut Department of Environmental Protection — state environmental agency.
- Connecticut Department of Economic and Community Development — state development agency, lead agency for Bryant site.
- Westinghouse Corporation — owner of Bryant Electric.

Background and Nature of Problem

Bridgeport's West End has historically been the heart of the city's economy, supporting over 60 industries within a half-mile radius. One of the main business anchors here was Bryant Electric, a Westinghouse-owned facility that produced circuit breakers and power panels for nearly a century. Housed in a mammoth four-story, 500,000-square-foot building, Bryant Electric employed more than two thousand people at its peak. In the 1980s, however, Westinghouse officials increasingly viewed the facility as functionally obsolete and prepared to sell it off.

When Bryant Electric finally closed down in 1988, the surrounding community took an immediate hit. "Having empty buildings like that in the neighborhood takes its toll on property values," says Kevin Gremse, economic development associate in the city's Office of Planning and Economic Development. One local business, Modern Plastics, had been operating for nearly 80 years across the street from Bryant Electric. In 1991, the company conducted $3 million in renovations. Two years later, the same property was assessed at half that value — $1.5 million. This is not surprising, says Gremse, given the company's location. "The Modern Plastics plant is surrounded by vacant, abandoned buildings like Bryant Electric. They are eyesores and they invite further decay, further abandonment, and further blight in the neighborhood."

The West End had been riding a downward spiral even before Bryant Electric closed its doors. Over the years, the area had become characterized by unkempt streets, eroding infrastructure, and rising crime rates. Many buildings were graffiti-covered while others were burnt and vandalized. In the 1980s, a group of businesses banded together and formed the West End Business Association. At monthly meetings, the group strategized about how to revitalize the area and encourage business growth. Steadily, they began to apply pressure on city officials. "Businesses were saying, 'You guys have to start doing something in the neighborhood because we're dying out here,'" says the city's Kevin Gremse. But the city was too mired in its own financial difficulties to help (Bridgeport actually declared bankruptcy in 1991). It wasn't until the Bryant Electric facility caught the attention of decision makers in Hartford, the state capital, that a comprehensive, state-funded strategy for the West End would emerge.

The irony is that despite the abundance of abandoned or under-utilized industrial buildings in the West End, there is actually a dearth of available land on which small businesses can grow — businesses that desperately need to expand if they are to survive. In fact, on the books, nearly 95 percent of Bridgeport land is developed or occupied. The city recognized that without public-sector intervention, many acres of "developed" yet idle industrial property would remain locked-up for years to come. With city involvement, on the other hand, this land could be freed for business expansion, a move that would simultaneously eliminate neighborhood blight and pave the way for economic resurgence in the West End. Local officials identified Bryant Electric as the first step in this process — "the linchpin to the West End's overall development plan."

In 1992, however, exactly four years after being closed, the Bryant Electric site was still on the market, with no buyers in sight. Westinghouse officials began to explore the idea of reusing the site themselves. They hired a nationally known consultant who proposed turning the existing building into a low-income housing complex — an idea that immediately drew fire from West End businesses and community groups. "It didn't make sense from an economic or social point of view," says the city's Gremse. "The project wouldn't have added to the local tax base. Plus, Bryant Electric was a huge building with no open land and no parking." In essence, there was simply no market and little demand for housing in this neighborhood; a housing project would have required expensive public subsidies to make it float.

What Westinghouse soon realized was that the property wouldn't move as long as the Bryant Electric building remained standing. The market for such mammoth, multi-story factories in urban settings was virtually dead. "In Bridgeport, a lot of our land contains these huge multi-story buildings," says Ed Lavernoich with the city, "but fewer and fewer companies want buildings like this. The demand for such sites here has just fallen through the floor. In addition, Westinghouse recognized that there were environmental problems with the property that would never be resolved as long as the building was standing." These lingering environmental concerns would ward off any potential buyers for the foreseeable future.

Meeting the Challenge

In 1993, officials from Westinghouse and the city sat down and began formally discussing options for the property. Westinghouse offered to turn the building over to the city, in its existing condition, for $1. City officials countered by saying they would take the building only if Westinghouse conducted all remediation and demolition. A compromise was reached. Westinghouse would handle all remediation; the city would then buy the property for $1 and conduct all demolition. As it turned out, because contamination was present underneath the building itself, remediation and demolition activities would occur simultaneously.

After conducting several studies, the city concluded that the Bryant Electric property should be promoted as a multi-use site. The plan involved the city demolishing the Bryant Electric building and acquiring an additional seven acres (approximately 30-40 properties) around the site, essentially forming a larger 12-acre industrial park. Existing structures would be demolished and remediation conducted only where necessary. City officials anticipated that only one or two sites would need extensive cleanup, at a cost of $500,000 or less.

The issue of funding was divisive from the outset. Because the city was emerging from bankruptcy, officials had to completely rely on state funds to pay for all site acquisition and preparation. The state, however, was reluctant to pour public funds into a speculative project — one that involved only tentative developers and tenants. "The state was afraid that work would be done and millions spent and no developers would be there," says the city's Gremse. "And we couldn't promise them that we'd definitely have a developer. But we *could* promise them that nothing would ever happen on those sites unless up-front work was conducted. The bottom line was: we needed to get the state to agree to let us take aggressive action. We were saying, 'Help us clean a site and we have great assurance that business will come.'" In the end, the city secured $10 million from the state Department of Economic and Community Development (DECD) and another $2 million in HUD Community Development Block Grants (CDBG).

Bridgeport's historic Bryant Electric building before demolition.

As plans for the project coalesced, opposition from historic preservation groups mounted. The Bryant Electric facility was listed on the National Register of Historic Places, and the Connecticut Historical Commission could not support its destruction without an identified reuse for the site. Peter Simmons from the DECD says, "It was difficult for the Commission to support tearing down one of the two biggest kingpins in the West End (the other being the Hubbell Building)." On the other hand, Simmons points out, "We couldn't get an end-user unless we tore down the building. It was a Catch-22, any way you looked at it." The DECD and the Historical Commission, fortunately, negotiated a creative solution. Instead of preserving the building, a report would be published on the history and significance of the West End district, which was to be distributed to libraries and schools statewide.

With the Bryant Electric project moving forward, plans for revitalizing the broader West End neighborhood also gained momentum. One of the key steps in this process was development in 1994 of a non-profit development group, the West End Community Development Corporation (CDC), that was comprised of area businesses, residents, local government representatives, and non-profit organizations. The CDC served as a hub for these groups, many of which had different goals and needs. “At the turn of the century, businesses and residents used to be one voice,” explains Tito Molina, executive director of the West End CDC. “But in the early 1970s, the decline of manufacturing drew adversarial relationships as people who used to work in these factories became unemployed.” Undercurrents of this tension persist today. “When you have industrial uses right up against residential uses, neither one wins,” says Ed Lavernoich with the city. “You have neighbors with incompatible missions.”

Through its work, the CDC sought to create a climate in which businesses and neighborhood pride could once again thrive. “We’re both a community confidence-building group and a municipal non-profit developer,” says Tito Molina. The CDC’s first priority has been to retain existing companies by improving area services, facilitating expansions, and enhancing the overall image of the West End. “When you try to attract customers to your store,” Molina says, “and there’s a burned-out car sitting across the street, people ask, ‘What’s wrong with this company? Why would they locate a business here?’” In just two years, the CDC has worked hard to alter this image.

Although the city secured $12 million to fund initial West End (and Bryant Electric) initiatives, more money clearly would be needed in the future. For a while, it appeared that a proposed Indian casino might fill this critical funding gap. Nearly 87 percent of Bridgeport residents supported the casino, which would have bolstered the city’s tax base and, in so doing, created a special economic development pool that would have generated millions annually. “That kind of revenue was essential to us in terms of infrastructure improvements,” says Kevin Gremse with the city, “and everyone was looking for something to happen that they could be proud of. They wanted an attraction that would make people *want to come* here.”

In November 1995, however, the state legislature shot down the casino proposal — a serious blow to Bridgeport. To counter this loss, Governor John Rowland pledged $25 million to the city annually for the next four years, a total of $100 million, for projects that could demonstrate a 1:3 ratio between state and private-sector funds spent. In other words, the state would give the city $1 for each $3 it could leverage in private investment. By summer 1996, the governor had earmarked the first $2 million of his $100-million pledge specifically for environmental cleanup at Bryant Electric (and surrounding properties), a project that is slated to attract at least $10 million in private investment.

Aerial view of Bryant Electric facility and West End neighborhood.

As of fall 1996, 90 percent of the Bryant Electric building had been demolished. The city reports that a world-class manufacturer (not yet publicly named) is hoping to move onto the site by December 1997. Although negotiations are still underway, the company plans to construct a 200,000-square-foot facility, with help from the city and the West End CDC, that will employ 300-400 people. The company will utilize the entire 12-acre industrial park created by the clearance of Bryant Electric and surrounding properties. But timing is critical for this project. If the deal drags out longer than anticipated, the purchaser may decide to relocate elsewhere.

The city and Westinghouse are currently working side-by-side at the site — the city handling demolition activities, Westinghouse dealing with all remedial issues. "In order to keep the project moving at a fast pace, we're overlapping — but not duplicating — our efforts," says DEP's Tom RisCassi, an environmental analyst involved with the site. "The setting is such that it would be difficult to handle the activities in a separate way." At the same time, the West End CDC has begun to acquire properties around Bryant Electric. Some sites were already in city hands through tax-foreclosure, while others are being purchased outright. The state worked with the city to develop a Municipal Development Plan which, once finalized, authorized the CDC to condemn properties through eminent domain. Environmental assessment is moving ahead on the parcels surrounding Bryant Electric with state and federal funds.

When site assessment is complete, Westinghouse will present a proposed Remedial Action Plan (RAP) to the state. Once the RAP is approved, provisions for a letter of completion (for Westinghouse) and a Covenant-Not-to-Sue (for the purchaser) may be addressed. "More investigation needs to occur," says DEP's RisCassi. "When the building is completely down and a RAP can be prepared, that will be the time to consider a Covenant-Not-to-Sue."

Although the end is still months away, this project has generated a great deal of optimism. "We're reusing the most significant property in the West End," says DECD's Peter Simmons. "For many years, it was the symbol of inactivity in Bridgeport and the West End. Redeveloping this property is not only a tangible demonstration of government-sponsored economic development; it also provides an opportunity for a suburban type site (with off-street parking and ample loading dock space) in an inner-city setting."

Regulatory Framework

The Bryant Electric facility is being addressed under Connecticut's Urban Sites Remedial Action Program, established in 1992, which operates in conjunction with the state's 1985 Property Transfer Act. The program is administered jointly by the Department of Economic and Community Development (DECD) for redevelopment issues, and by the Department of Environmental Protection (DEP) for environmental issues. Projects are selected based on economic potential and remedial feasibility.

Bryant Electric is classified as a Type I site because there is an identified responsible party (Westinghouse) willing to remediate the site. As with all Type I sites, DEP and DECD are providing expedited review and approval of voluntary cleanup proposals. After Westinghouse officials submitted the initial application, they launched a site investigation to assess the extent of environmental contamination. As of fall 1996, site investigation is still being done in conjunction with demolition. When the site assessment is finished, Westinghouse and DEP will negotiate a Remedial Action Plan.

In January 1996, the State of Connecticut adopted new remediation standards that address different contamination scenarios, including direct exposure, contaminated soil mobility, and volatilization from groundwater. Under the direct exposure scenario, the state has developed two sets of numerical standards for soil cleanup — one set for residential areas, one for contaminated soils in industrial/commercial areas. To address mobility, the state also has issued additional cleanup standards for contaminated soils with respect to groundwater quality. Connecticut differentiates between groundwater that is presumed to have been impacted by development and groundwater that is presumed to be unimpacted and which, therefore, may be available as a drinking water source. A third scenario addresses volatile organic compounds in groundwater. The new regulations establish numeric criteria for groundwater that is contaminated with volatiles and is located less than 15 feet below a structure or building.

Once remediation is complete at the Bryant Electric site, the DEP plans to issue Westinghouse a letter acknowledging completion of activities. The Commissioner of Environmental Protection may enter into a Covenant-Not-to-Sue for the new owner(s) of the remediated property.

Financing

Westinghouse has absorbed over $1 million in site remediation costs to date, with the remaining expenses being shouldered by the public sector. In 1992, the city secured $2 million in federal Community Development Block Grant (CDBG) funds — a special "economic development" grant that was in addition to the city's usual $4 million annual allocation. "Through our congressional office we learned that there was a leftover pile of money targeted for economic development," says the city's Gremse, "so we put together an application right away." An additional $10 million from the state Department of Economic and Community Development (DECD) was earmarked for site acquisition and demolition in the West End. Of the total $12 million, $4 million was handed over directly to the West End CDC, with the remaining $8 million being administered by the City of Bridgeport.

Another funding source was secured recently when Governor Rowland committed $25 million annually to the city for the next four years (backed by state bonds), for a total of $100 million, to projects where there could be a demonstrated 1:3 ratio between state and private-sector funds spent. By summer 1996, the first $2 million was dedicated specifically to the neighborhood (for demolition and remediation) and is slated attract at least $10 million in private investment from the targeted end users.

Private lending institutions have not been involved with this project to date. However, once remediation is complete and the purchaser receives a Covenant-Not-to-Sue, banks have expressed interest in financing the second phase of the process — the actual redevelopment. According to a report by one city contractor, "Interviews with heads of major utilities and financial institutions show that there is strong interest in supporting the West End revitalization process. Both the banks and the utilities are prepared to work with the city and the state to develop a program of incentives that can expand, relocate, and create business."

Impacts

Peter Simmons of the state DECD says that the current developer negotiating with the city plans to bring 300-400 jobs into the area. This would translate into a $20-$50 million investment in the West End, including equipment and machinery. "We want to make sure that this is going to be the anchor of West End development," Simmons says. "It's certainly the most important project for that area. We want to do it right."

The city is moving ahead with plans to construct a new West End police station that will overlook the Bryant Electric industrial park. The new 8,000-square-foot station will house roughly one third of the Bridgeport's police force. That site is undergoing environmental assessment and will be acquired by the CDC in late fall 1996. A major West End business, the Bodine Corporation, also is expanding its factory space onto seven properties now being assembled by the CDC.

In addition, the CDC has developed a program called "Operation Clean Sweep" that provides street cleaning and trash clearing services for West End businesses by employing needy neighborhood residents. Under a $200,000 contract, the Kuchma Construction Co. assembles and trains a five-person maintenance crew of workers identified by the Family Services Woodfield social service agency. "This is a fee-for-service program," says the CDC's Molina. "For companies that can't conduct routine maintenance, such as mowing their lawns, we'll offer them services below [market prices]." Molina adds that this has already evolved into an effective job training program. "In the first six months," he says, "half our crew have been able to 'graduate' and move on to more permanent employment."

Lessons Learned

According to participants involved with this project, redevelopment of the Bryant Electric plant was facilitated by the following:

Involvement by the City to Offset the Project's High Remediation Costs

"From a pure real estate standpoint, no one's interested in this type of project," says the city's Kevin Gremse. "It doesn't make sense." To illustrate this point, Gremse offers some figures from the project. Westinghouse has spent over $1 million on remediation, while the city has spent $700,000 on demolition, personnel costs, and site preparation. Expenses on this four-acre parcel, therefore, totaled roughly $2 million, or $500,000 per acre. Gremse points out that an average four-acre *clean* parcel in the West End would be one quarter that price, or $125,000 per acre.

"We've identified an end-user and put together a site plan based on what that company wants to see," says Gremse. "But due to the high mil rate here [the property tax rate], the lease price is expected to be higher than in surrounding towns," says Gremse. "So we've had to [work to] level the playing field as much as possible."

Strong Community Involvement

The CDC's improvements in the neighborhood have caused a ripple effect throughout the rest of the community. Tito Molina notes that companies now are painting their buildings, assuming a new pride in the appearance of their properties. "That's the leveraging effect of this work — people see improvement [in the neighborhood] and are therefore willing to invest further at their own companies," he says. "People sense that we've turned the corner, that we've weathered the worst of the storm, and that better days are ahead."

Molina adds that it is critical to establish credibility as a neighborhood-based organization. It is important, he argues, to be able to relate to a wide range of different groups: community residents, government officials, and businesses. "You have to be able to go in and out of these different worlds," Molina says. "You have to...feel comfortable going into a low-income housing project and also sitting down with a CEO and talking hard business."

State Efforts to Streamline and Expedite Brownfield Projects

Many brownfield projects are stymied by long time frames and high costs associated with site preparation and remediation. The key to making these sites competitive with greenfields is to reduce these time frames and costs without compromising environmental protection. Referring to the Bryant Electric site, Bridgeport's Kevin Gremse notes, "Companies were not going to commit themselves to a project when there was such a loose time frame" associated with cleanup and site preparation.

To tackle this problem, the state has attempted to streamline permitting and oversight activities. The Connecticut Department of Economic and Community Development (DECD), which provided financial and technical assistance, acted as the liaison between DEP and DOT. "We dedicated staff and helped expedite the project," DECD's Simmons says. "That's our function — to make sure needs are met without excessive cost or time delay." Kevin Gremse adds, "Hopefully the lessons learned through this process will allow us to do it more quickly in the future."

Promulgation of New Soil Cleanup Standards

"Before 1996 there was no set regulatory level," says DEP's Tom RisCassi. "The new cleanup standards establish a target — specific numbers and criteria to guide the work." According to Peter Simmons of the state DECD, "The new standards make cleanups less complicated and more achievable, something that has significantly eased our ability to recycle brownfield sites back into the community. Under the old rules, we couldn't meet cleanup standards at a cost that was economically feasible. That [encouraged] developers to go out to farmlands and set up operations there — something that nobody wanted."

Presence of a Strong and Vocal Business Community in the West End

In the 1980s, the West End Business Association formed to advance the interests of companies in this neighborhood. According to Tito Molina of the West End CDC, "This is really the driving force behind the healthy business climate here and, in my opinion, the catalyst for the turnaround of the West End. Long before the city developed a vision of rebuilding the manufacturing base, the Business Association had developed such a vision." Molina has sought to incorporate some of the Business Association's momentum into the CDC. "I'm convinced that the future rests in retaining and growing small family businesses. They live around here and have root systems here. I look at that as a real opportunity. If you can accommodate them, they will produce for you."

Bryant Electric as the "Proving Ground" for Bridgeport's City-Wide Brownfield Program

According to Mike Freimuth, director of Bridgeport's Office of Planning and Economic Development, Bryant Electric was a proving ground for city-wide policies aimed at addressing brownfield reuse. "We have five million square feet of obsolete industrial space in Bridgeport," Freimuth says. "For the most part, it has been rejected by the marketplace. Bryant became the forerunner on how to deal with this real estate."

Some of the key barriers that city officials encountered at Bryant Electric included: (1) proving the economic obsolescence of the site in order to justify its demolition (especially in light of its historical importance); (2) contending with environmental contamination; and (3) striving to adopt a land use plan that spurs *area-wide* redevelopment, rather than simply addressing one site.

To make the Bryant Electric project a reality, says the city's Freimuth, "we realized that we had to become very proactive. In the past, we [tended] to wait for deals. This, on the other hand, was more of a speculative deal; we created the market as we went along. [We learned that] you need to get out in front — get ahead of the curve — and do land clearance and cleanup. At that point, the marketplace will have the comfort it needs." City officials have identified four basic steps that help facilitate brownfield reuse, steps that are now guiding city brownfield policy:

- prioritize sites based on redevelopment potential;
- initiate discussion with current owners or operators;

- work with the community to determine the site's best use; and
- actively market sites.

Contacts

Kevin Gremse
(203) 576-7603
or Ed Lavernoich
(203) 576-7221
Bridgeport Office of Planning and Economic Development

Peter Simmons
Engineer
Connecticut Department of Economic
and Community Development (DECD)
(860) 258-4230

Tom RisCassi
Environmental Analyst
Connecticut Department of
Environmental Protection (DEP)
(860) 424-3781

CIRCLE F FACTORY
Trenton, New Jersey

Key Players

- City of Trenton — local government.
- Lutheran Social Ministries of New Jersey — developer and general partner for the housing project.
- Circle F Civic Association — local community organization.
- Nat West Bank (Fleet Bank, as of May 1996) — lender and investor for the housing project.
- American Properties Corp. — company that sold the residential parcel to the City of Trenton; maintains ownership of industrial portion of property.

Background and Nature of Problem

For more than 100 years, a family-owned plant — that began as the Trenton Watch Company and later became a manufacturer of electrical components known as the Circle F factory — was the heart of a small working class neighborhood in Trenton's East Ward. Starting in the late 1970s, however, the factory changed ownership several times, finally ending up in the hands of American Properties Corporation (APC), a New-York based real-estate holding firm. APC owned the Circle F property, but the factory operator was Liberty Lighting Company — a firm, according to APC's Jamil Simon, that was reputed to engage in shady business dealings. In 1990, Liberty Lighting Company went bankrupt and the Circle F factory closed down, leaving a gaping hole, both physical and psychological, in the neighborhood.

The following year, the City of Trenton designated the Circle F neighborhood a Neighborhood Preservation Area, and embarked upon a program of community rebuilding. Trenton's Neighborhood Preservation Program receives approximately $70,000 in state assistance annually, and the city matches these funds with upwards of $50,000 per year. A strong civic association was formed, and a variety of improvements — including housing rehabilitation, sidewalk replacements, and tree plantings — were initiated. However, without a strategy to address the abandoned Circle F plant, which occupied an entire city block in the heart of the neighborhood, the area's long-term stability could not be ensured.

In 1992, the city initiated negotiations with APC, the owners of the factory. Reuse of the site would be complicated because the facility had been constructed in two phases. Roughly half the site (on Monmouth Street) was occupied by a variety of long and narrow multi-story buildings built between the 1880s and 1930s, while the other half contained a single large, roughly square, concrete structure built in the 1950s. The former was not conducive to industrial activity but could support residential use. The latter was potentially attractive for an industrial user but, due to the building's configuration, would not be suitable for residential use.

"It was clear to APC that we would never rent the Monmouth Street building for industry again," says APC's Simon, "and that if there was any value in that property, it was for residential use. We realized that we were not the best company to do a housing project."

Meeting the Challenge

After several negotiations with APC, the City of Trenton decided to purchase the residential building on Monmouth Street, while APC retained the balance of the site for industrial use. The city spent $15,000 to subdivide the property, which involved relocating utilities and constructing a wall to separate the two parcels. As part of the transaction, APC agreed to carry out site-wide environmental remediation that was required under New Jersey's Environmental Cleanup Responsibility Act (ECRA), which was still in effect at the time of the transaction. Following the cleanup, the New Jersey Department of Environmental Protection issued a Letter of Completion, certifying that the work had been carried out in accordance with an approved plan.

Simultaneously, the city had been working with a manufacturer of canvas swimming pool covers, Merlin Industries, which had outgrown its quarters elsewhere in the city and was thinking of leaving the area. The city and neighborhood both considered the firm, which was committed to hiring local residents and generated little noise or pollution, to be ideally suited for an industrial building surrounded by residential homes. In 1993, the city was able to facilitate an agreement under which Merlin moved into the portion of the Circle F factory that was designated for industrial use, occupying roughly half of the available industrial space. Later that year, a printing company rented the remainder of the building for storage.

Residential redevelopment of Trenton's Circle F factory on Monmouth Street.

Throughout this process, the city had been working closely with the neighborhood organization, the Circle F Civic Association. After exploring a variety of options, the city and the association agreed that the most appropriate use for the residential portion of the site would be senior citizen housing. "Senior housing really stabilizes a neighborhood," says Doug Hughes, neighborhood preservation coordinator with the City of Trenton. Based on that decision, the city in 1994 issued a Request for Proposals seeking a qualified team to develop the building for senior citizens. As part of the selection process, three finalists made presentations to the Civic Association, and members of the association had the opportunity to tour projects previously developed by the teams. After a thorough review process, the city selected Lutheran Social Ministries (LSM) of New Jersey, an experienced non-profit developer, to undertake the project.

In June 1995, LSM applied for and received an allocation of federal Low-Income Housing Tax Credits, as well as state capital subsidy funds. Later that year, when the city and LSM inspected the property in greater detail, they found that major environmental cleanup tasks remained, including extensive removal of lead-based paint as well as limited removal of asbestos and polychlorinated biphenyls (PCBs) in old lighting fixtures. Since the previous owner had received a Letter of Completion from the State of New Jersey, Trenton officials could not pursue APC for these "surprise" cleanup costs, which totaled over $450,000. Instead, the city and LSM picked up the tab. "We were definitely annoyed when we started discovering that stuff," says Alan Mallach, director of Trenton's Department of Housing and Development, "but then we just decided, 'let's get on with it, we don't have a leg to stand on' in terms of cost-recovery." For their part, APC officials argue that the company fully complied with New Jersey cleanup laws. "Discovery of lead-based paint shouldn't have been a surprise," says Jamil Simon with APC. "It's just a fact that when you redevelop older buildings, you are going to have lead paint problems."

Remediation took place during the fall of 1995, and rehabilitation of the Circle F factory for 75 senior citizen units began before the end of the year. The rent for a one-bedroom apartment is slated to be $350, a very affordable rate for downtown Trenton. Residents are expected to move into the new housing complex, which will include a variety of health care and support facilities, early in 1997.

Regulatory Framework

The project was initiated in 1993, when New Jersey's Environmental Cleanup Responsibility Act (ECRA) was still in effect. Later that year, the state legislature replaced ECRA with the Industrial Sites Recovery Act (ISRA). The state issued a Letter of Completion to American Properties Corp. for environmental remediation conducted in accordance with ECRA.

Financing

The Circle F project involved a series of complex financing arrangements. When APC announced that it was selling off the portion of the property designated residential, many purchase offers — some in the $500,000-$600,000 range — were submitted by development companies in the area. But APC preferred to work with the city, sensing that it was "in the best position to secure public approvals and the financing needed to make this project a reality," according to APC's Simon. The city agreed to pay $15,000 to subdivide the property; in return, APC agreed to sell the building to the city for $200,000. The firm also agreed to finance the deal with a ten-year mortgage, which requires no payment of principal by the city during the term of the loan and interest payments only after the third year. As such, there were no initial out-of-pocket costs for the city, which simply held the property while APC paid the taxes. The agreement stipulated that, at the time of site redevelopment, Trenton officials would pay APC the $200,000, which they did.

Lutheran Social Ministries (LSM) explored many public and private financing options for building the senior housing units. Even before construction had begun, LSM paid upwards of $500,000 out of its own coffers for site exploration, demolition, and remediation activities. "It was a risk," admits LSM vice president, Reverend Stanley Steele, "but we felt comfortable with it, and confident that things would work out." Things did pan out when LSM teamed up with Nat West Bank (Fleet Bank, as of May 1996), a financial institution with a strong interest in low-income housing projects. The bank gave LSM approximately $4 million in construction loans, then joined up with the non-profit to form a "limited partnership," which would be eligible for Low-Income Housing Tax Credits. "We have a strong program for buying Low-Income Housing Tax Credits," says Nat West's Rick Lawten. "It is one form of Community Reinvestment Act (CRA) activity that can be very profitable." The

Community Reinvestment Act, promulgated in 1977, requires that banks make an effort to invest in and accommodate the credit needs of their local communities.

Under a limited partnership, the investor has 99 percent ownership in the venture and the general partner has 1 percent ownership. But, in practice, the general partner has total control over the project. In this case, Nat West Bank agreed to be the "investor," and LSM established a for-profit subsidiary to act as the "general partner." In 1995, the limited partnership applied for and received Low-Income Housing Tax Credits, which formed the crucial piece of financing for this project. Low-Income Housing Tax Credits were authorized by Congress several years ago as an incentive to attract private capital to housing projects developed for lower-income residents; in essence, they help minimize investment risk and shore up the investor's rate of return. In the case of Circle F, state officials determined that the building would qualify for $800,000 in Low-Income Housing Tax Credits per year, beginning in 1997 when the facility opens, and ending in 2007. Total tax credits over this ten-year period would be $8 million. Because Nat West financed the project up front with approximately $4 million, the bank will see a considerable yield (approximately 12 percent) on its investment. "I'd like say it was altruism," Nat West's Rick Lawten says, "but, in fact, the capital structure, the quality of the participants, and the market are what made this an appealing project."

Impacts

The Circle F project has been a major success story for the City of Trenton. Rehabilitation and reuse of the factory — and strong community involvement in the process — has had a positive impact on the neighborhood. This success builds on the groundwork laid by the Neighborhood Preservation Program, which for years has worked to improve streets and basic infrastructure throughout Trenton. The process illustrates the city's creative approach to the remediation and reuse of brownfield sites (e.g., allowing multiple uses, residential and industrial, to take place within a single site). As a result, a formerly derelict building with major importance to the surrounding community was restored to active use, and once again is serving as a strong centerpiece to the neighborhood's vitality.

Thus far, city officials say, the residential project alone has resulted in a $7.5 million infusion of funds to the local community. LSM's Reverend Steele points out that the neighborhood will see ongoing benefits, as well. "When the houses are built," he notes, "all the people that live there will walk two blocks down and use the services there, buy their doughnuts there. It's a continuing investment."

The industrial portion of the Circle F property also has been a success. "In the past three years, Merlin Industries has grown tremendously," says APC's Simon. "They started with 14 employees and now have 90."

Lessons Learned

According to participants involved with this project, redevelopment of the Circle F factory was facilitated by the following:

High Level of Comfort Among Project Participants

The redevelopment of the Circle F factory illustrates how a project can be successful when many critical players become comfortable with each other. In this case, there was a willing lender/investor, a competent and highly respected developer, an active citizens group, and a committed city agency to oversee the process. "We were attracted to Lutheran Social Ministries," says Nat West's Lawten. "They had a good development team, excellent architects, a successful track record in health care facilities and low-income housing, and they are stable financially." Reverend Steele states that "this project fit well with our mission of serving the needs of low-income, elderly people." Neighborhood residents were clearly supportive of the project; the Circle F Civic Association had been involved in every step of decision making, and had made the final selection of LSM as the developer. And finally, because the city was confident that the key pieces were in place for a successful deal, officials were willing to lend time, expertise, and public funds for the project.

The Circle F redevelopment was not a simple job, though. It involved multiple stakeholders and a complex set of issues — which required a massive juggling act for those involved. The key, according to Reverend Stanley Steele, was not throwing in the towel when problems arose. "In our case," he says, "the buildings did not automatically lend themselves to housing, and we were always finding surprises in terms of lead paint or structural problems. At the same time, we were trying to keep the numbers down as low as possible, trying to establish a level of comfort for our lenders and investors." It was a balancing act that required determination and a strong conviction that, in the end, the investment would pay off.

Strong Commitment by Trenton Officials

Trenton officials made the Circle F project a reality by committing city resources at the outset. For projects like this, where the profit margin often is not large enough to attract many developers, local government may be the only player with the financial resources and legal authority (as well as the credibility) to make a project happen. "If the city had not taken a proactive role in pulling this deal together," says the city's Mallach, "the building could still be sitting there empty. I think this is an important point to make, particularly at a time when the importance of local government — and its key role in bringing about meaningful change — is underestimated."

Use of Federal Low-Income Housing Tax Credits

The Circle F project points to the effectiveness of Low-Income Housing Tax Credits as a tool for encouraging brownfields redevelopment. Because of the program, it was possible — and profitable — for Nat West Bank to back a project from which it might have retreated otherwise.

Contacts

Allan Mallach
Director
Department of Housing and Development
City of Trenton
(609) 989-3504

Reverend Stanley Steele
Vice President
Lutheran Social Ministries (LSM) of New Jersey
(609) 585-0400

American Axle Plant and Northeast Buffalo Parkway
Buffalo, New York

Key Players

- Buffalo Enterprise Development Corporation — local non-profit development agency.
- Buffalo Department of Community Development — local agency responsible for redevelopment of brownfields.
- American Axle & Manufacturing — corporation that spurred redevelopment and transportation improvements in the railway corridor.
- New York State Department of Transportation — state transportation agency.
- Consolidated Rail Corporation — company selling rail right-of-way.

Background and Nature of Problem

At the turn of the century, Buffalo boasted the second largest rail center in the country after Chicago. With the explosion of the automotive industry in the early 1900s, the city was poised to become a major player since rail lines allowed raw materials and finished goods to be received and shipped to automotive assembly plants around the U.S. and Canada. "Throughout Buffalo, industrial facilities were built up around rail lines, the primary mode of transit at the time," says Dave Stebbins of the Buffalo Economic Development Council (BEDC), the city's non-profit development agency. "Then around the plants you had neighborhoods where the workers traditionally lived. Industrial facilities in the middle of neighborhoods — it was typical of Northeast Buffalo."

In recent years, however, industrial needs for the city have changed. Following a national trend, many of the old manufacturing firms in Northeast Buffalo have either shut down or moved out to the suburbs in search of cheaper rents and new facilities. Another factor contributing to this exurban migration is the fact that rail transport — once the dominant and preferred mode for industry transport in

Buffalo — no longer plays such a critical role. Truck transport now has firmly taken its place. This change poses a serious problem for Northeast Buffalo in terms of retaining existing businesses and attracting new ones: the neighborhood is characterized by small and winding streets, built during the horse-and-buggy era, that are inaccessible in today's fully loaded eighteen-wheelers.

The flight of industry from Northeast Buffalo has taken its toll on the surrounding community. Once stable neighborhoods are now marked by vacant lots and abandoned houses. The old railroad tracks through the community have become a weedy and overgrown corridor that serves as a magnet for illegal dumping and crime. By some estimates, roughly 75 percent of the land (40 acres) around Consolidated Rail Corporation's (Conrail's) corridor is vacant or underutilized. "The physical condition of...Conrail lands and surrounding vacant parcels could at best be characterized as dilapidated and unkempt," writes De Leuw, Cather & Co., the city's planning consultant.

Northeast Buffalo was anchored for decades by the presence of two major General Motors (GM) factories. Unfortunately, the GM-Harrison plant on Clyde Ave. closed in 1990, leaving a gaping hole — physical, emotional, and economic — in the neighborhood. The other stalwart, the GM-Saginaw Division on E. Delavan Ave., had been plagued with financial concerns for years and faced an equally grim future. The neighborhood desperately needed new life, but it was unclear how or when that would ever happen.

Meeting the Challenge

The turnaround occurred sooner than most expected. In February 1994, American Axle & Manufacturing purchased the former GM-Saginaw Division on E. Delavan Ave (as well as another facility in the nearby town of Tonowanda) and continued producing automotive axles. According to *Automotive Industries* magazine, within a matter of months American Axle was reporting solid profits at the once struggling facility. One thousand jobs were retained, and an additional 600 were brought on board. Company officials pledged to invest nearly $100 million at the E. Delavan Ave. site, with first priority being construction of a new $25-million paint facility. But there was a caveat. Without improved truck access to the site, American Axle could not follow through with its plans to increase operations and bring on new employees.

Fortunately, American Axle's needs dovetailed with the current thinking among Buffalo planners. Over the years, city officials had come to recognize that their infrastructure — particularly urban highways — needed revamping if Buffalo was going to compete with suburban greenfield industrial areas that have better access to the interstate highway system. "If we want to attract other businesses to the inner city, we need to be able to move their products from the neighborhood streets to the expressways," Mayor Anthony Masiello told *The Buffalo News* in 1994. "We want to do everything we can to help [American Axle]. They are an existing strength on the East Side which we should build upon."

But, says Dave Stebbins of the Buffalo Enterprise Development Corporation (BEDC), "we didn't want to stop with American Axle. Besides these two GM plants, there are properties all along the old Conrail corridor in Northeast Buffalo that are inactive or abandoned. We realized there was no good access, especially for these smaller facilities that need to drive trucks through narrow city streets. We needed to re-engineer our basic infrastructure from rail to highway."

So as American Axle moved forward with its expansion plans, the city launched its own parallel initiative to revitalize the surrounding neighborhood. The centerpiece of its plans called for converting Conrail's defunct rail beds into roads that would be equipped to handle larger truck traffic. City planners developed a three-part initiative that included: 1) creating an access road along Conrail's old corridor; 2) attracting businesses to the vacant/underutilized parcels along the corridor; and 3) integrating pedestrian bikeways and greenways to the plan.

The project is divided into three phases, the first two of which have been approved and funded. Phase 1 involves building a road — known as the Northeast Buffalo Parkway — between the American Axle site and the Kensington Avenue Expressway. Phase 2 will extend the Northeast Buffalo Parkway to the former GM-Harrison Plant on E. Amherst Street. Phase 3, which is still in the planning stages, would involve constructing interchanges on the existing Kensington Expressway. Thus far, the city has secured $6.5 million to cover the first two phases. In 1995, the New York Department of Transportation (DOT) committed $3.5 million for Phase I from Industrial Access Program funds. For Phase 2 of the parkway, $3 million has been secured from a variety of state and federal sources.

In fall of 1995, American Axle brought its new paint facility on line at E. Delavan Ave. Meanwhile, the former GM-Harrison plant, empty for nearly four years, had been purchased by a local developer for "close to nothing," according to BEDC's Dave Stebbins. The site now contains a 300,000-square-foot light industrial park that will house a range of warehousing and distribution facilities. The new owner already has secured several tenants and plans to attract many more. Within the next two years, American Axle and Harrison Industrial Park will be connected by the new parkway, forming a new business corridor that city officials hope will spur further development in the surrounding area.

Throughout the summer of 1996, the city and Conrail were negotiating the sale of the 26-acre rail corridor, the site of the proposed Northeast Buffalo Parkway. BEDC's Dave Stebbins estimates that the price will end up "somewhere in the $200,000-$300,000 range." The parcel has undergone complete environmental assessment and only minor contamination problems were found, as city officials anticipated. Construction of the first two phases of the parkway — from the American Axle facility to the Harrison Industrial Park — is slated to begin in early 1997 and finish within the year. The plan calls for providing buffering between the new parkway and nearby residences. "It doesn't take long to actually build the road," says BEDC's Dave Stebbins. "What takes so long is all the 'soft stuff,' applying for grant funds, designing the plans, etc."

But even when the road is complete, the city's efforts are far from over. "The first step is building the Parkway," says Dave Stebbins of the BEDC. "The next step is to assemble property along the corridor and develop a 15-acre business park that will include a small business incubator." Towards this end, BEDC has purchased and plans to market several public and privately-held parcels. "Many older industrial properties here have been abandoned as industries move out to suburban greenfields," says Stebbins. "We look at this whole corridor as one big brownfield area."

Regulatory Framework

American Axle entered New York's Voluntary Cleanup Program (VCP) in order to clean up a portion of the old Conrail tracks. Launched in 1994, the VCP provides a "release from liability" to parties that have successfully remediated an enrolled property.

Financing

American Axle's significant private-sector investment — over $100 million in the E. Delavan Ave. facility — has leveraged a torrent of public dollars for improvements in Buffalo's Northeast neighborhood. The city has raised $6.5 million from general revenue bonds to cover construction of the Northeast Buffalo Parkway, a highway that will hopefully attract business back to this economically depressed area. In 1995, the New York DOT committed $3.5 million for Phase I in Industrial Access Program funds. "Normally the Industrial Access Program funds are a 60 percent grant/40 percent loan program," says Dave Stebbins of BEDC. "But American Axle went to [then] Governor Mario Cuomo and personally asked for a special budgetary line item. It was special in two regards: first, it was not the usual 60/40, but rather a 100 percent grant; second, it was $3.5 million, significantly more than the usual limit of $1 million."

Three million dollars in public funds were secured for Phase 2 of the new Parkway. The city recently approved $1 million in general revenue bonds; $1 million was secured in Enterprise Community funds (the City of Buffalo was awarded $3 million in federal Enterprise Community funds, which the state fully matched); and $1 million was raised through Section 108 loan guarantees from the U.S. Department of Housing and Urban Development (HUD). Section 108 loan guarantees enable localities to issue debentures in order to cover the cost of projects, pledging their annual HUD Community Development Block Grant (CDBG) funds as collateral.

In addition to funds specifically earmarked for the parkway project, the area around the Conrail corridor is part of a newly designated state Economic Development (ED) Zone. The two-square-mile ED Zone contains American Axle, the new Harrison Industrial Park, and portions of the Conrail corridor. Similar in concept to the federal Empowerment Zone/Enterprise Community program, the state ED Zone program provides for growth-based activities a wide range of tax credits, including investment tax credits, sales tax credits, and utility discounts. "The tax credits are only for new jobs or new utilities, in other words, growth-based activities," explains Dave Stebbins of BEDC. "The company has to be planning to expand. So it becomes an incentive for companies to locate within the zone." Stebbins adds that American Axle is one of the first companies to be certified to receive tax credits in this new ED zone.

When asked why Buffalo didn't pursue federal highway funds, Stebbins replies, "All federal funds must be funneled through the Niagara Frontier Transportation Council, a regional planning organization. It involves requesting funds through five-year Transportation Improvement Plans, and the bottom line is, we needed more immediate action than that."

Impacts

American Axle has given new life to Northeast Buffalo. Dick Dauch, president of American Axle & Manufacturing, told *Automotive Industries* in June 1995, "This place used to make 9,000 to 10,000 axle and driveline systems a day. Now we're at 14,000. And our investments for new machinery still haven't kicked in. So if you're asking how we're making money, it's because we're producing 30 percent more with the same equipment."

With American Axle's $100-million investment, the city successfully leveraged over $6.5 million in public dollars. The impact of this investment already is visible. Officials speculate that the new Harrison Industrial Park complex, built on the former GM-Harrison site, could generate an additional 200 jobs in the near term and as many as 1,000 jobs down the road. The area will need to support 150 more truck shipments daily, which only reinforces the need for the new parkway. Two major tenants planning to locate in the Harrison Industrial Park (who would have brought in 600 new jobs) were lost due to inadequate truck/vehicular access.

According to BEDC's Dave Stebbins, the city also has mapped out impacts for the entire Northeast Buffalo area. Officials estimate that the parkway project will trigger a slew of development, including several hundred thousand square feet of new industrial space, 1,000-1,500 manufacturing jobs, upwards of $6 million in public investment, and $50 million in private investment.

Lessons Learned

According to participants involved with this project, redevelopment of the American Axle site and construction of the Northeast Buffalo Parkway were facilitated by the following:

Private Investments

In the late 1980s and early 1990s, Buffalo's Northeast side, the city's prime industrial district, was mired in a spiral of economic decline. Yet when American Axle in 1994 committed over $100 million to the former GM-Saginaw plant, the situation turned around almost overnight. American Axle is now the centerpiece of the city's revitalization efforts — helping to leverage state dollars for transportation improvements and attracting other viable businesses to the area. "Here came this company that invested over $100 million in the city, buying the American Axle plant, refurbishing it, providing job training — just a huge commitment," says Dave Stebbins. "You know, it made us realize: if they can believe in the city, then there must be something really important here." American Axle's investment prompted the city to move forward with long-overdue highway improvements in the neighborhood — improvements that were critical if the city was ever going to attract businesses to this economically depressed area. "American Axle was the private sector kick-in-the-pants to get this project moving," says Stebbins, "but now its grown bigger than that."

Strong Public-Private Partnership and Coordination Among Different Layers of Government

"The public/private partnership was the key to this project's success," says BEDC's Dave Stebbins. "It's demonstrated by the fact that American Axle, United Auto Workers (UAW), Conrail, and the city were all behind the project — everyone worked together. There was also cooperation among different levels of government. We had commitments by a democratic governor (Mario Cuomo) followed by a republican governor (George Pataki), so you can see that it crossed party lines."

Monthly Planning Meetings

Monthly planning meetings between the key players — American Axle, Conrail, the state DOT, and the City of Buffalo — were instrumental in making sure the project moved forward. "The meetings were the incentive to keep the project going," says BEDC's Stebbins. "Problems could be identified and dealt with on a regular basis."

Creative Public Financing

The first two stages of this project have been funded by a wide range of public-sector sources, including state transportation department bonds, federal/state Enterprise Community (EC) funds, Section 108 loan guarantees, and general revenue bonds backed by the city. That such varied funding sources can be secured illustrates the popularity of brownfield reuse projects among public officials. Brownfield redevelopment is seen as an effective way to tackle numerous issues concurrently (i.e., environmental remediation, transportation improvements, housing, economic development, neighborhood revitalization, and historical preservation). As such, decisionmakers increasingly are willing to divert scarce dollars toward these high "bang-for-the-buck" projects.

Contacts

Dan Barry or Dave Stebbins
Buffalo Enterprise Development Corporation (BEDC)
(716) 842-6923

ERNST STEEL SITE
Cheektowaga, New York

Key Players

- New York State Departments of Environmental Conservation and Health — state agencies overseeing project.
- Benderson Development Company — redeveloper of several sites in Cheektowaga.
- Town of Cheektowaga — local government overseeing project.
- Erie County Industrial Development Agency — industrial development body that worked with Benderson to facilitate deal.

Background and Nature of the Problem

The Ernst Steel Corporation operated for over 30 years at a plant in Cheektowaga, New York, a once rural town located just outside the Buffalo City line. Closed down in 1980, the facility changed hands several times, finally being owned by U.S. Metal Source in 1991. By this time, the Buffalo suburbs had sprawled outwards, completely surrounding the plant. "Cheektowaga was becoming a highly developed commercial mall area," says Craig Slater, attorney for Harter, Secrest and Emery, representing the Benderson Development Corporation. This trend was sealed in the early 1990s with construction of a massive shopping mall called The Galleria, which became one of the most successful commercial retail developments in western New York. Town Supervisor Dennis Gabryszak notes, "The Galleria changed the face of Cheektowaga." Now this once-sleepy town supports a population of 100,000 and over 90 percent of the available land is developed.

With this explosion of growth, Ernst Steel and several other nearby industrial properties became anomalies — and glaring eyesores — in their new surroundings. The Ernst site contained several huge black buildings with "tupelos," large triangle-shaped air vents, perched on the roofs. The property was also known to possess environmental contamination from 30 years of assembling, servicing, and painting steel parts. The company had routinely dumped waste products — including lead-based paint, metal shavings, iron oxide dust, and machine-cutting oil — out back in the low-lying portions of the property, causing serious lead and chromium contamination in soils.

Site assessments conducted between 1986 and 1994 confirmed the presence and location of these hazardous substances. Eventually, the property was assigned a 2a classification under the state's Registry of Inactive Hazardous Waste Disposal Sites — a temporary classification for sites having inadequate or insufficient data. In 1992, the New York State Department of Environmental Conservation (NYSDEC) and U.S. Metal Source negotiated a cleanup and signed a formalized Consent Order. U.S. Metal Source removed 80 cubic yards of contaminated soil and concluded that an additional 1,000 cubic yards still remained at the site. But the cleanup came to a screeching halt when, later that year, the company declared bankruptcy.

Meeting the Challenge

Two years later, in 1994, Benderson Development Company bought the ten-acre Ernst Steel site out of bankruptcy court. "Location — that's why we were interested in this property," says Craig Slater, adding that his client also secured a low price. "It was a really good opportunity," agrees Martin Doster of NYSDEC. "This project doesn't fit the typical mold of a 'brownfield project' because local government wasn't the driver — the market drove this one, more specifically, proximity to The Galleria drove it."

As Benderson was negotiating its purchase of Ernst Steel, the company bought another property across Walden Avenue — a weedy and overgrown lot that housed a former trucking operation. Benderson had plans to construct a new hotel, Hampton Inn, on the property, and it contacted the Erie County Industrial Development Agency (ECIDA) to discuss possible tax breaks for the project. "Essentially, the developer asked us for funding and tax abatements [for the hotel] and we were not supportive," says ECIDA's executive director, Ron Coan. "We *would* have funded a hotel to support a downtown cluster or an airport cluster. But, under normal circumstances, we just don't think the public sector should finance something that's so clearly a private-sector [endeavor]."

ECIDA and Benderson continued talks for a few months until a deal was struck: If Benderson moved ahead and remediated the Ernst Steel site, ECIDA would provide the tax breaks Benderson wanted for the Hampton Inn project. The deal included an 80 percent tax abatement on value-added property taxes to county and town jurisdictions (in this case, a substantial amount, since the property was an abandoned lot beforehand), sliding down to 50 percent by year ten. Sales taxes also were abated during the entire construction period. "Yes, the area is giving up future tax revenues," says ECIDA's Ron Coan, "but we're getting a prominent developer to clean up a huge brownfield site, and, in the long run, we'll receive lots of sales tax proceeds from the facility, which is pure profit for the community."

In 1995, the Ernst Steel site was given a formal Class 2 designation on the state's Registry of Inactive Hazardous Waste Disposal Sites, a classification that means the site poses a significant threat to human health and/or the environment, and action is required. Later that year, Benderson brought in a consulting firm to further sample and analyze soils at the Ernst Steel site. The consultant determined that 70-80 percent of the contaminated soils exceeded state regulatory levels and would need to be treated and removed from the site — the main culprit being dispersed lead paint chips. State cleanup guidance documents dictated that leachable lead and chromium could not exceed 5 milligrams per liter, and total lead could not exceed 500 parts per million (ppm). The consultant also determined that contamination was present on an adjacent property that was previously owned by Ernst Steel and sold to Delevan Industries in 1976. Benderson decided to buy this six-acre property as well, essentially joining the two cleanup projects together.

Later in 1995, Benderson submitted an Interim Remedial Measures (IRM) Removal Action Plan for both the Ernest Steel and Delevan Industries sites, which the NYSDEC quickly approved. Interim Remedial Measures are conducted at sites where a source of contamination or an exposure pathway can be effectively addressed before the site is thoroughly investigated. Essentially, this means that site assessment, demolition, and facility construction may occur simultaneously (in some cases, construction actually may be part of the remedial activity). Because of these overlapping activities, "it was an extremely difficult cleanup," says Craig Slater, attorney for Benderson Development.

"In brownfield cleanups, every shovel-full of soil you dig up is expensive, so we try to limit the number of shovels of dirt and sampling points," says Slater. "In this case, we ultimately failed — the remediation was nearly eight times greater than we expected [because of the lead paint]. But we found an experimental technology" to help defray the remediation costs. What Benderson used was a hydrogen sulfide liquid treatment that ended up saving the company an estimated $300,000 in cleanup costs.

The hydrogen sulfide process involves feeding contaminated soil into a machine on site. Inside the machine, hydrogen sulfide binds with the paint's lead constituent, rendering it immobile. "What concerns us about toxics is that they move," explains Slater. "If they don't move, it's okay." Slater indicated that, after receiving hydrogen sulfide treatment, soils at the Ernest Steel site passed the EPA's Toxic Characteristic Leaching Procedures (TCLP) test, meaning that the toxics were no longer mobile and, therefore, were rendered non-hazardous. Benderson, therefore, was able to dispose of Ernst Steel's 2,500 tons of soil at solid waste landfills, not hazardous waste landfills — a move that saved big money for the company (tipping fees are $350/ton for hazardous waste; $45-$50/ton for solid waste).

The Ernst Steel site has railroad tracks running behind the property, on the other side of which are residential homes. "People there were happy because this huge black building was being taken down," says Town Supervisor Dennis Gabryszak. "Their only complaint during demolition and cleanup was about the dust. [In accordance with DEC oversight], Benderson made adjustments."

The actual cleanup began in December 1995. As of summer 1996, Benderson had completed 70 percent of this remedial work and planned to submit an IRM Closure Report within the next few months. Once the state receives the Closure Report, according to NYSDEC's Doster, it will take approximately six months to "de-list" the site. Meanwhile, on the remediated portions of the site, two tenants (Target and TGIF Restaurant) have signed leases and are open for business. Benderson reports that 90 percent of the tenants for the neighboring Delavan Industries site have been identified.

Reflecting on this project's success, Craig Slater, attorney for Benderson Development Company, says, "My client [Benderson] isn't afraid of very much. They have nerves of steel and are exceptionally smart. They seldom give much thought to cleanup. If the location is right, we will buy it and find a way to make the cleanup worthwhile. In the case of the Ernst Steel site, we had a lot of problems and [cost overruns], but still we made it work."

"This project is a win-win scenario," notes the NYSDEC's Marty Doster. "We're getting this land back on the tax rolls and getting rid of an eyesore at the same time." Dennis Gabryszak, town supervisor, agrees: "Ernst Steel definitely is a success story. It adds to the local tax base, creates jobs. Plus there are many future benefits — the project helps leverage future redevelopment initiatives."

Regulatory Framework

New York's Voluntary Cleanup Program (VCP), launched in fall 1994, is administered by NYSDEC. However, cleanup at the Ernst Steel site did not proceed through the state VCP. Instead, the project adhered to New York Superfund regulations. The developer will receive a "final closure" letter indicating that when the Closure Report is submitted and approved by the state, Benderson is officially finished with the site cleanup.

Financing

The Ernst Steel project was completely financed by Benderson Development Company. "We don't bring in banks until our properties are off the State's Registry of Inactive Hazardous Waste Disposal Sites. When the Ernst Steel site is removed, by March 1997, the banks will get involved," says Craig Slater, attorney for the Benderson Development Company. Essentially, this means that while Benderson financed all initial costs, the developer will mortgage the property with a bank when cleanup and remediation are complete.

Impacts

Redevelopment of the Ernst Steel property "is definitely going to create jobs and have a positive economic impact," says Town Supervisor Dennis Gabryszak. "Also, it will be a big aesthetic improvement" over the property's former condition. The Target store will provide 50 construction jobs, and, when operational, officials estimate there will be 150 full- and part-time jobs. Sales taxes alone from the Target store and TGIF restaurant will be $1 million per year. Property taxes will be upwards of $300,000-$500,000 annually.

While the project has many benefits, it also is possible that the Town of Cheektowaga may experience some growing pains. "When you look at this area, there's The Galleria, K-Mart, Target, and all these other shopping centers. Cheektowaga is the retailing capital of western New York," says Gabryszak. "If people want to shop, this is where they come. But you have to wonder, at some point in time, whether some of these stores may get in trouble. What's the economic viability of all of them surviving so close together?"

Gabryzsak adds that while Cheektowaga for years focused on "development strategies," now the town must begin focusing on growth management and reuse of old properties.

Lessons Learned

According to participants involved with this project, redevelopment of the Ernst Steel site was facilitated by the following factors:

Strong Partnership Between NYSDEC and the Developer

Craig Slater, Benderson's attorney, emphasizes that NYSDEC officials were instrumental in the redevelopment of the Ernst Steel site. "Time can kill a job," says Slater, "and they didn't allow that to happen. These guys literally killed themselves to help us meet construction deadlines. It's evidence of their willingness to partner with business to redevelop sites."

Benderson's Ability to Spread Risk Among Different Brownfield Projects

"Benderson views brownfields as the last frontier on which to make money," says Slater, Benderson's attorney. The company's large size offers two distinct advantages: first, it can afford to fund large projects without involving banks; second, because it has multiple projects going on at once, it essentially can spread out the risks associated with any one of them.

ECIDA's Creative Tax Abatement Plan

ECIDA struck a deal with Benderson Development Company: If Benderson would remediate the Ernst Steel site, ECIDA would provide tax breaks for development of the hotel project. It was a creative financing tool that benefitted both Benderson and the Town of Cheektowaga. Benderson was able to move on two projects simultaneously — both of which have proven profitable — while the town eliminated a glaring eyesore and fostered development of numerous commercial enterprises.

Contacts

Martin L. Doster, P.E.
Regional Hazardous Waste Remediation Engineer
Division of Environmental Remediation
New York State Department of Environmental Conservation
(716) 851-7220

Craig Slater, Esq.
Harter, Secrest, and Emery
(716) 853-1616

THE ROUNDHOUSE PROPERTY
(Harlan & Hollingsworth Shipyard)
Wilmington, Delaware

Key Players

- Lammot Dupont Copeland, Associates International — the roundhouse property seller.
- Raybold Group — the roundhouse purchaser.
- Delaware's Department of Natural Resources and Environmental Control — the state oversight agency.
- U.S. Environmental Protection Agency — federal environmental agency.

Background and Nature of Problem

Wilmington's Harlan & Hollingsworth Shipyard was founded in 1836 to manufacture passenger railway cars. By the 1870s, the company was nationally known, having expanded to more than 40 acres on the Christina River. The facility included about 60 buildings in which high-quality railroad cars, iron-hulled steamers, stationary steam engines, and boilers were produced. The shipyard launched 70 ships during World War I and then closed down due to lack of work. It was reopened in the early 1940s to produce landing craft and other small ships used during World War II, before closing again in the 1950s. At that time, the Harlan & Hollingsworth Corporation was liquidated and the property sold off to various entities.

Since the heydays of Harlan & Hollingsworth, the Wilmington waterfront has witnessed steady economic decline. Many of the old shipyard buildings are now underutilized or abandoned altogether. What was once a source of pride and economic vibrancy is now marked by junkyards, warehouses, and empty lots. The city has sought for years to redevelop this downtown waterfront area, but a series of plans have fallen through due to lack of funds.

In 1992, Delaware's governor stepped in and appointed a Blue Ribbon Task Force to make recommendations concerning the future of the Brandywine and Christina Rivers. Within two years, the group had fashioned a bold plan called "A Vision for the Rivers," outlining measures to improve environmental quality, enhance wildlife habitat, increase recreational opportunities, encourage economic development, as well as preserve historical, cultural, and community attributes along both river corridors. "This is more than the renaissance of the Wilmington waterfront," wrote the task force. "It is the creation of a new focus of pride, excitement, and employment that all Delawareans can relate to and become a part of."

One of the old Harlan & Hollingsworth shipyard buildings was a wooden railroad roundhouse on 1.6 acres in the heart of the old industrial district. The roundhouse was a half-moon shaped building into which trains entered and rotated on a turntable, enabling operators to direct them into one of 21 buildings for storage. Idle since the 1950s, the property had fallen into disrepair. It was one of several properties owned by Lammot Copeland, Jr., president of Associates International, Inc. Copeland had bought the property in 1984 and used it for storage of printing and graphic arts materials. In the late 1980s, he placed the roundhouse on the market but no buyers surfaced for several years.

"There were problems selling it," says Copeland. "I'm not sure how much of it was related specifically to potential contamination problems, but certainly that was a factor. Also, the building may have discouraged some people — they didn't want to deal with demolition and questions about [underlying] contamination." In 1995, Copeland himself tore the building down.

Historic rendering of Wilmington's Harlan & Hollingsworth Shipyard.

Meeting the Challenge

Not long after Copeland demolished the roundhouse, he received an offer on the property from Jerry Heisler of the Raybold Group, who had plans to build a self-storage warehouse on the site. The sale was contingent, however, upon completing all environmental assessments and obtaining liability waivers under Delaware's newly enacted brownfields program.

In November 1995, the prospective buyer and seller met with Department of Natural Resources and Environmental Control (DNREC) officials and an environmental consultant in order to map out a strategy for the sale. Copeland agreed to enter Delaware's voluntary cleanup program (VCP) and learned he could defray site assessment costs through the newly-enacted Brownfields Assistance Act program. But the state saw an additional opportunity to help Copeland save costs. Karl Kalbacher, program manager at DNREC, contacted the U.S. Environmental Protection Agency (EPA) and discussed whether federal Superfund dollars could be dedicated to the roundhouse property.

In fact, DNREC had been drawing on Superfund dollars for brownfield assessment activities along Wilmington's waterfront for nearly a year. In the early 1990s, the department had been searching for ways to encourage reuse of more than 70 old, industrial properties in this area. Uncertain site conditions warded off prospective buyers, fueling the cycle of economic decline. Under the traditional state Superfund program, DNREC would have looked at each site individually — an extremely costly and time-consuming operation. On the other hand, by conducting an area-wide assessment of the waterfront, the department could shuttle multiple sites through the system in a cost-effective manner. DNREC officials settled on the idea of completing several region-wide Preliminary Assessments, or Brownfields Preliminary Assessments I, that covered land tracts as large as 200 acres, with as many as 70 different property owners. Where necessary, DNREC would follow up with Site Investigations (Brownfields Preliminary Assessments II). In 1994, DNREC asked EPA Region III to support its initiative with allocation of "Pilot Dollars" under the Delaware-EPA Superfund Cooperative Agreement. EPA responded positively, and, since then, has committed roughly $250,000-$350,000 annually for brownfield site assessment work. "EPA officials nationwide are looking for direct success stories," says DNREC's Kalbacher. "They are looking to spend dollars where they can see direct creation of jobs and taxes and, equally important, an improvement to the environment."

In the case of the Harlan & Hollingsworth roundhouse property, DNREC envisioned that site assessment costs would be shared between the seller and the state (using its federal Superfund dollars). Both parties benefitted from the collaboration. "The state was able to piggyback on the work we were doing with our property," says Copeland, "so it was a saving to them, and they paid for some work that we otherwise would have had to fund." An environmental consultant for the project adds, "The state was able to get data from the site that it needed but that we *didn't* need."

In the winter of 1996, samples were collected and taken to the state's mobile lab for screening. The primary contaminants found were low levels of polycyclic aromatic hydrocarbons (PAHs) and lead. For remediation, DNREC determined that construction of a cap — in this case, placing asphalt over the entire site — would serve as an adequate barrier for the underlying contamination. "That form of containment will satisfy our requirements," says DNREC's Kalbacher. A deed restriction will be placed on the property indicating that it's suitable for commercial and industrial use only.

When most of the sampling was complete, Copeland applied in May 1996 for reimbursement under the state's recently enacted Brownfields Assistance program. Administered by the Delaware Economic Development Organization, the program provides matching funds for up to 50 percent of site investigation expenditures. In this case, Copeland hoped to recoup half the $37,000 he had spent. "The preliminary word is that they are looking upon our application favorably," says Copeland.

By fall 1996, the cap was in place, and DNREC issued the seller, Lammot Copeland, a Certificate of Completion of Remedy. The buyer, Jerry Heisler of Raybold, was given a formal Covenant-Not-to-Sue. Although the purchase price was not disclosed, Copeland indicated that he was able to sell the property at the fair market value for a clean parcel.

"I think we've been fortunate on a couple of different fronts," says Copeland. "First, there were no horrendous surprises at the site. A good bit was known about the [environmental conditions] because of sampling done on nearby parcels. It was more a case of confirming what we expected to find. Second, Delaware's brownfields legislation has been incredibly helpful. Without it, Jerry [Heisler] would have been much more anxious about getting involved."

Despite smooth sailing to date, one glitch has surfaced that could derail the project altogether. It turns out that Delaware Department of Transportation (DOT) officials, in an effort to rejuvenate the Harlan and Hollingsworth Shipyard area as part of the "Vision for the Rivers" initiative, are seeking ways to improve public access to the waterfront area. Existing roads are narrow and winding, not suitable for truck transport or heavier traffic patterns. Two of the three proposed plans would carry a new traffic artery smack through the old roundhouse property site. "We're not sure what's going to happen," says Copeland. "This is still up in the air." In the meantime, Copeland and Heisler are moving towards the closing with their fingers crossed.

Regulatory Framework

Delaware's voluntary cleanup program (VCP), in place since 1993, is run by the Delaware Department of Natural Resources and Environmental Control (DNREC). DNREC requests an application from the interested party and, upon approval, drafts a simple, generic agreement that includes a walk-out provision for both parties and no penalty provisions. Cleanup parties may enter the program before or after the site investigation stage, but not after the remedial plan stage. Upon DNREC's approval of the investigation conducted at the site, the party submits a work plan. Remedial activities are conducted with departmental oversight in order to ensure that cleanups are carried out in accordance with DNREC regulations.

In Delaware, parties have two options for selecting appropriate cleanup levels for the site. First, they may apply "trigger" levels derived from the EPA Region 3 Risk-Based Concentration Tables for nearly 600 chemical contaminants (using a 10^{-6} risk reduction for cancer-causing chemicals and a Hazard Index=1 for non-carcinogens). Sites with contamination above trigger levels are required to perform further investigation, while sites below those levels (in both soil and groundwater) may receive a No Further Action letter from DNREC. Alternatively, the party may choose to apply site-specific cleanup standards based on a site's future land use. As with the roundhouse property, DNREC may allow the use of institutional or engineering controls (e.g., construction of an asphalt cap) to achieve acceptable levels of remediation. Cleanups must achieve a 10^{-5} health-based risk assessment.

Liability protection for prospective purchasers also is available under the Hazardous Substance Cleanup Act (HSCA), provided the purchaser signs a VCP simple agreement and completes the remediation of property with the department's oversight. Upon completion of site remediation, the department issues a Certificate of Completion (CoC) of remedy, providing a release from liability to prospective purchasers. Current and past owners and operators of sites also may receive a CoC; however, the CoC does not release them from liability. In the case of the roundhouse, the CoC reflects a No Further Action determination, with the department maintaining the option to re-open the site if conditions substantially change and warrant further investigation or remediation. New owners of remediated property also are given contribution protection under the HSCA. While CoC letters do not shield a party from federal enforcement action, an unwritten agreement between EPA Region 3 and DNREC reduces the possibility of federal involvement at sites enrolled in Delaware's VCP.

Financing

In 1995, the State of Delaware passed legislation providing two forms of brownfield financial assistance. The first is the Brownfields Assistance Fund, which provides matching funds for up to 50 percent of site investigation costs, up to $25,000, where there is a presumed environmental problem and a clear development plan for the project that will employ new workers. This money is not available for state, county, or municipal entities; it is strictly for private-sector groups. In this case, Copeland applied to the Delaware Economic Development Organization and is hoping to recoup half the $37,000 he spent assessing the roundhouse property.

The second program, the Brownfields Tax Credit program, piggy-backs on existing legislation that provides tax credits for "green industries," including recycling operations, certain banks, and clean-manufacturing facilities. The new tax credits are available for individuals who build or renovate a building located on a brownfield and *where new workers are hired.* In targeted census tracts, the program offers a 90 percent graduated tax credit against gross receipts that expires after 15 years; non-target census tracts provide a reduced percentage for ten years. For corporations, the state offers a $500 tax credit per year for each new employee and a $500 tax credit for every $100,000 of capital investment. Because the roundhouse property is in the former category, the buyer, Jerry Heisler of Raybold, will be able to take advantage of these substantial tax credits. According to DNREC's Karl Kalbacher, a medium-sized retailer such as Heisler could see nearly a 50 percent return on initial investment.

Impacts

If all goes well, the roundhouse property is slated to be transferred from Lammot Copeland to Jerry Heisler in late fall 1996. By that time, it will be fully paved as part of the site remedy. Heisler will then proceed with construction of his self-storage warehousing facility, which will create several new jobs. DNREC estimates that the facility will bring significant economic benefits to this waterfront area.

Lessons Learned

According to participants involved with this project, redevelopment of the roundhouse property was facilitated by the following:

Enactment of Delaware's Brownfields Legislation

Delaware's brownfield program has been in place since 1993, but actual legislation was not passed until 1995. This new law provides a great deal more certainty and closure to the process — something that proponents argue will trigger heightened site reuse throughout the state. "The law was very definitely a major reason why this project was a success," says Associates International's Lammot Copeland. Kalbacher says the liability provisions "represent real opportunities to save costs and provide closure to the process."

Strong Public/Private Cooperation

The strong public/private partnership was essential to the success of this project. Lammot Copeland indicates, "There was a willingness among the three parties involved — myself, Jerry Heisler, and DNREC — to work out a reasonable and acceptable program."

Innovative Use of Federal Superfund Dollars for a Brownfield Project

"We were using Superfund dollars for site characterization and redevelopment rather than first pursuing enforcement," says DNREC's Karl Kalbacher. Kalbacher emphasizes that this arrangement benefitted both the property seller, Lammot Copeland, and the state. The seller got help because EPA picked up part of the site assessment tab; the state gained because site characterization at the roundhouse property helped fill in data gaps for their region-wide assessment of the Wilmington waterfront. "Using Superfund dollars is a creative tool," says Josie Matsinger, assistant brownfields coordinator for EPA Region 3. "It's an avenue that states can pursue, and it seems to be the direction that people are taking."

Development of an Overall "Vision" Guiding Redevelopment Initiatives

The "Vision for the Rivers" initiative provided the blueprint for redevelopment along Wilmington's waterfront. "In the beginning, a lot of people said 'yeah, right, pie-in-the-sky, this will never happen,'" says environmental consultant, Marian Young. "But since then, there have been many meetings with the architects to try and get people thinking. The planners don't expect people to go out and build the exact plan they've created — they just want something that people can look at, something to help them all sing off the same page."

Many people believe that the $100-million "Vision for the Rivers" initiative will succeed because, unlike previous plans, it has buy-in from key elected officials. "There's endorsement from the highest levels of government — both U.S. senators, the former and current governors, and members of the House of Representatives — in addition to the business community," says DNREC's Kalbacher. "The key is that the Vision has been marketed well. First, you create the vision; then you market it so everyone's supportive; then you prioritize activities. This is exactly what they're doing." Former Delaware Governor Russell W. Peterson told the *News Journal* in 1994, "We are...proud of our vision of what the Wilmington waterfront can be: an exciting place to live, work, and enjoy life. This vision provides a great opportunity for our community."

Capitalization of Wilmington's Key Asset — Access to the Waterfront

Cities around the country are launching redevelopment initiatives that capitalize on key assets and natural features, most notably waterways and/or nearby mountains. Wilmington is no exception. "We now recognize what great assets the Brandywine and Christina and their tributaries are," former Governor Russell W. Peterson told the *News Journal* in 1994. "We must do much more to capitalize on these assets...In so doing we can improve the quality of lives, particularly that of our children and grandchildren." What also seems to be true is that plans capitalizing on waterways and other natural attributes attract strong community support, a key ingredient for any brownfield project's success.

Contacts

Karl Kalbacher
Program Manager
The Site Investigation and Restoration Branch
Division of Air & Waste Management
Department of Natural Resources
and Environmental Control (DNREC)
(302) 323-4540

OREGON MILL SITE CONVERSION PROJECT
Seven Counties in Oregon

Key Players

- Rural Development Initiatives, Inc. — non-profit development organization; lead public-sector partner for this project.
- PacifiCorp — third largest investor-owned utility west of the Rockies; lead private-sector partner for this project.
- U.S. Bank of Washington — commercial lending institution; project partner.
- Stoel, Rives, Boley, Jones, and Gray — law firm; project partner.
- Economic Development Administration — federal economic development agency; project partner.
- U.S. Environmental Protection Agency — federal environmental agency; awarded Rural Development Initiatives $200,000 Brownfield Pilot Site grant.
- Oregon Economic Development Department — state agency; project partner.

Background and Nature of Problem

In the early 1990s, mounting public concern over protection of forest ecosystems in the Pacific Northwest, coupled with legal challenges under the Endangered Species Act, forced a policy shift within the U.S. Forest Service. The agency announced major scale-backs in allowable harvests of timber from federal lands — reductions that aimed to protect the environment. What these policies could not protect were communities whose livelihoods were linked directly to the forests. In Oregon, alone, over 120 timber mills closed, resulting in the loss of approximately 55,000 jobs statewide.

For many of these rural towns, mill closures wiped out the primary source of employment, income, and local tax revenues, leaving residents economically and psychologically devastated. This loss was compounded by the fact that many former mill sites possess some environmental contamination, a stigma that actively discourages their redevelopment. As is the case with urban brownfields, potential purchasers and investors are reluctant to get involved because of concerns about liability, cleanup, and time delays. Many of the former mill sites remain idle and undeveloped to this day.

In January 1993, President Bill Clinton and Vice President Al Gore convened the Northwest Timber Summit to devise a forest management plan that would simultaneously advance environmental protection and economic growth in the region. One promising result of the meeting was a series of government assistance programs, collectively known as the Northwest Economic Adjustment Initiative, that were designed to spur redevelopment in the wake of mill closures. The Economic Development Administration (EDA), within the U.S. Department of Commerce, received in its 1994 appropriations an additional $16.4 million in Title IX economic adjustment assistance grants for timber-dependent communities. Congressional members, recognizing that future job creation in these towns hinged on productive reuse of the mill sites, urged the EDA administrator to "favorably consider" grant applications geared towards redevelopment of such properties.

Meeting the Challenge

One application that EDA received during the summer of 1994 was from a public/private partnership that sought to redevelop seven former mill sites in Oregon. EDA awarded the initiative — known as the Oregon Mill Site Conversion Project — $366,000 in grant money to launch environmental assessment and community outreach at the sites. EDA, in the process, became an official "partner" in the project. Other partners included: the Oregon Economic Development Department (OEDD); Rural Development Initiatives, Inc. (RDI), an Oregon-based, non-profit development organization; PacifiCorp, the third largest investor-owned utility west of the Rockies; U.S. Bank of Washington; and the law firm of Stoel, Rives, Boley, Jones, and Gray. RDI is the official project management entity; its non-profit status makes the initiative eligible for federal funding.

The goal of the Mill Site Conversion Project was to transform the seven sites into productive, readily-usable industrial or commercial parcels. Lessons learned from this experience, the partners envisioned, would be applied to other rural areas facing similar mill closures. Within the first year, the project aimed to complete the following activities: (1) assessment of environmental conditions at the seven properties; (2) identification of appropriate cleanup strategies (including assessment of costs); and (3) community outreach. The project's ultimate goal was to develop for each of the seven properties detailed site plans, known as "master plans," that would articulate ideal end-uses based on remedial requirements, financial factors, and input from local communities. With these master plans in hand, site owners then would be able to market their parcels or secure financing more effectively.

Astoria Plywood Cooperative, located at the mouth of the Columbia River.

The seven participating communities were selected by a consultant for Rural Development Initiatives. The consultant initially identified 25 communities with well-established local economic development organizations and invited those communities to complete surveys. (Certain other sites were not considered because of concerns about the viability of future development, low community support, or weak leadership.) Each of the 25 communities responded to a standard set of questions, and, based on their responses, the consultant selected seven communities to participate in the program. The communities include: Astoria, Coquille, Grants Pass, Myrtle Creek, Philomath, Sweet Home, and Merlin.

Mill owners had several reservations about involvement with this project, the primary concern being: if environmental contamination was discovered at their site, would they be exposed to unforeseen regulatory action? To allay these fears, the partnership in 1994 crafted formal Memoranda of Understanding (MOU) with mill owners, clearly outlining roles, responsibilities, and legal protections. The MOUs established that, even if contamination was uncovered at a site, participants were free to exit the program at any time without fear of state enforcement action. "We made sure that the private partners, including the powerful PacifiCorp, were there at the negotiating table for these MOUs," says Dana Peck, manager of the Mill Sites Conversion Project. "If it hadn't been for the private partners, I think many of the mill owners would have balked."

When all the MOUs were signed, RDI and the mill owners began introducing the project concept to local community leaders. RDI facilitated the creation of community-based redevelopment teams, called Local Action Committees, which met bi-monthly to discuss redevelopment options. Local Action Committees were comprised of a wide range of stakeholders, including civic groups, government agencies, private-sector companies, non-profit organizations, and environmental interests.

At the same time, RDI hired environmental consultants to conduct Phase I site assessments, including wetland delineations and flood plain evaluations. All seven sites were found to contain wetlands — some having only minor acreage, others having significant land area in wetlands. Assessments revealed hydrocarbon contamination to be the most frequent contaminant. While all sites demonstrated some redevelopment potential, infrastructure improvements were necessary across the board. Many sites possessed only rudimentary water and sewer service, and would require upgrading for future development. Several also needed transportation access improvements, such as new turn-off lanes or road relocations (as of fall 1996, discussion of these measures was underway with the Oregon Department of Transportation).

The seven sites possessed a range of challenges and opportunities. The Philomath and Sweet Home properties both are owned by corporate entities with potential internal capacity to fund some cleanup. The Grants Pass property is controlled by an operating trust with limited incentive to conduct extensive cleanup. Myrtle Creek is owned by an entrepreneur with a strong interest in cleanup and development of the site. The Merlin site until recently was held by Miller Redwood, a corporate timber entity; RDI's environmental assessment of that property revealed only minor contamination, which Miller Redwood remediated before selling the site in fall 1995 to a developer, who developed the site for use as a rock-crushing operation in conjunction with a nearby gold mine.

The Coquille site is a former Georgia-Pacific mill that closed down in 1990. For several years, Coquille officials were eager to see this prime industrial property returned to productive use. But, says RDI's Dana Peck, city officials also realized that "Georgia-Pacific could sit on its property and pay taxes forever rather than go through change-of-ownership, risking discovery of site contamination in the process." Georgia-Pacific finally did turn the property over to the City of Coquille in the early 1990s and agreed to pay up to $1 million in site remediation costs. By 1994, when the property was included in the Mill Site Conversion Project, Coquille officials were planning to redevelop the site using a combination of funding from Georgia-Pacific and the OEDD. The site is enrolled in Oregon's Voluntary Cleanup Program (VCP) and has undergone site assessment but has not been remediated. State officials anticipate that cleanup expenses will be minor — much less than the $1 million Georgia-Pacific committed.

The Astoria Mill, formerly owned by the Astoria Plywood Cooperative (a worker-owned cooperative), went bankrupt in the early 1990s after defaulting on a $3.2 million loan from the Small Business Administration (SBA). The SBA currently holds a lien for that amount on the property. Officials from the City of Astoria, intent on redeveloping the site, have requested that SBA wave (or substantially reduce) the lien and transfer the property to city hands. However, the city is not willing to take title and assume liability until all remediation activities at the site are complete.

The Astoria site presently is enrolled in Oregon's Voluntary Cleanup Program (VCP). Nearly $1 million in cleanup has been conducted at the property. The first $500,000 was provided by the Oregon Department of Environmental Quality (DEQ), the second

$500,000 was funded by the city, backed by a loan from the ShoreTrust Bank. ShoreTrust Bank is a financial partnership formed in 1995 between U.S. Bank of Washington, the Shorebank Corporation of Chicago, and a Portland-based conservation group called Ecotrust. ShoreTrust provides financial backing to groups involved with environmental protection and community development. "The types of businesses ShoreTrust is interested in are not viewed as good risks by conventional lending institutions," EcoTrust's Ted Wolf told Portland's *Daily Journal of Commerce* in 1995. "That's not because the people and businesses involved are not trustworthy, but because the businesses aren't familiar and don't fall within a familiar lending category." Astoria officials plan to repay ShoreTrust Bank's half-million dollar loan with revenue generated from the redeveloped mill site. How the site will be reused remains a question. The community is divided between support for commercial retail use and support for industrial use.

One year into the Mill Site Conversion Project, in summer 1995, RDI received two additional pieces of funding. The first came from the U.S. Environmental Protection Agency (EPA), which awarded the group a $200,000 Brownfields Pilot Site grant — money that primarily is being used to develop master plans for the seven sites. The master plans attempt to weave remedial requirements into feasible reuse plans for each site. For example, where a property contains a contaminated hot spot, the master plan might call for placement of a structure or paved surface to eliminate exposure pathways. These plans offer tangible ways that the sites could be redeveloped — something that will help to market them effectively.

The second piece of funding was from EDA, which committed an additional $300,000 to the Mill Site Conversion Project. The money primarily would be used to develop generic remedies for common pollutants found at the seven sites. The hope was that generic remedies would greatly expedite cleanups and reduce costs. In addition, EDA's grant is supporting creation of a computer model designed to help communities weigh the relative costs and benefits of a development. For a given project, the model might factor in necessary public expenditures for infrastructure improvements, compared with anticipated revenues.

By summer 1995, the Local Action Committees from the seven mill communities had articulated possible options for reuse of their sites. The most popular was industrial/commercial activity, such as a business park. These "community preference" lists guide formation of the master plans and should facilitate the marketing of the sites. "It is one of the most important things for a company that's contemplating locating in one of these towns," Peck says. "Of course, they have to be guaranteed a good labor force and core amenities for company executives, but a receptive community is critical." RDI is exploring the idea of giving commercial real estate firms exclusive rights to market the sites, a move that might encourage the firms to aggressively locate end-users.

Of the seven sites, two — Astoria and Merlin — have changed hands (only Merlin has been remediated). Both of these properties soon will be redeveloped. With the exception of Astoria, which required a $1-million cleanup, officials expect that costs for remediation at the remaining sites will be quite low. Currently, RDI is reviewing applications for Round 2 of the Mill Sites Conversion Project. This phase, launched in January 1996, will target five additional sites for redevelopment, bringing the total number of enrolled sites to 12.

Regulatory Framework

Two of the sites in this project, the Astoria and Coquille properties, are enrolled in Oregon's Volunteer Cleanup Program (VCP). Under the VCP, parties may receive liability exemption through a Covenant-Not-to-Sue, but more often the Oregon Department of Environmental Quality (DEQ) issues No Further Action Required letters, which limit, but do not completely eliminate, liability. The Astoria and Coquille sites both will be issued No Further Action Required letters. The DEQ has funded Phase I and Phase II assessments for both these sites. In addition, DEQ paid $500,000 of the cleanup costs at the Astoria site. The Merlin site was remediated, but not under the state VCP.

Financing

PacifiCorp's subsidiary, Pacific Power and Light, an electric utility operating in seven western states, led the private-sector partners involved with the project. "PacifiCorp serves more timber-dependent communities than any other utility in the country," says RDI's Dana Peck, "and the viability of those communities has a real effect on the company's profitability, so [PacifiCorp] is willing to commit resources towards that end." The utility company committed staff time to assist in project management, site planning, and technical and financing assistance. It also was instrumental in recruiting other private-sector partners, such as U.S. Bank and the law firm of Stoel, Rives, Boley, Jones, and Gray, whose contributions are listed in the table below.

Public-sector partners provided a key piece of financing for this initiative. The EDA awarded RDI between 1994 and 1996 a total of $666,000, which was used for initial site assessment activities, community outreach, development of generic remedies, and creation of master site plans. The Oregon Economic Development Department (OEDD) dedicated over $100,000 in staff time to assist in the redevelopment of the seven sites.

Several other public-sector entities contributed to this project, but were not official "partners." The EPA, for example, awarded RDI a $200,000 grant under its Brownfield Pilot Site program in summer 1995. EPA funds were dedicated towards finishing the development of master site plans. The City of Astoria, backed by a loan from ShoreTrust, contributed $500,000 to clean up its site; the state DEQ financed the remaining $500,000. Oregon's Division of State Lands and the U.S. Army Corps of Engineers provided substantial assistance with wetland issues and related regulatory requirements.

Contributions from public and private partners that backed the Mill Site Conversion Project are listed below. Note: figures below are only for the entities that officially "sponsored" this project.

Contributions From Public/Private Partners

Firm	Description	1994-1995	1995-1996
PacifiCorp	Direct cash contributions, project management, and staff assistance.	$74,500	$32,500
Stoel, Rives, Boley, Jones, and Gray	In-kind legal service.	$27,500	$2,500
U.S. Bank	Evaluation and cost-benefit analysis services.	$21,500	$12,500
Oregon Economic Development Dept.	Site Work	$50,000	$53,000
EDA	Grants	$366,000	$300,000
TOTAL		**$539,500**	**$400,000**

SOURCE: "Mill Site Conversion Project for Oregon: Final Report," Rural Development Initiatives, Inc., February 1996.

Impacts

According to Dana Peck, project manager for the Mill Site Conversion initiative, "We're about a year ahead of the schedule I'd anticipated for the properties." Two sites already have changed hands and several others should be cleaned and redeveloped by fall 1997.

The Mill Sites Conversion Project has identified and quantified environmental issues at the seven designated properties, thus eliminating the uncertainty that often accompanies brownfield sites. Vague concerns surrounding the environmental issues of the former mills now have solid technical answers.

Lessons Learned

According to participants involved with this initiative, the Mill Site Conversion Project has been facilitated by the following:

Strong Public/Private Partnership

One of the key aspects of this project was the public/private partnership that grouped together funding, staff support, and technical assistance. The partnership streamlined and facilitated activities such as site assessment, zoning, resolution of environmental liability, and redevelopment planning. It also fostered a sense of trust with participating mill properties. "There wasn't a sense of two people sitting on opposite sides of the table," says RDI's Dana Peck. "Instead, we just had informal conversations about the properties. A real partnership feeling developed over time."

Despite the partnership's success to date, RDI still believes that communication between the various public and private entities could have been stronger. The project has required complex coordination between the many partners to effectively handle the myriad environmental, financial, and community issues at each location. In the future, to streamline interaction with multiple state agencies, RDI hopes to work with a single "brownfield coordinator" (likely within the Oregon Economic Development Department), who would serve as the hub of information for the state. "Our hope," says RDI's Peck, "is that the coordinator will essentially provide one-stop shopping at the state level."

Public Outreach and Community Involvement

This project illustrates the importance of mobilizing local residents when reusing brownfield sites. The redevelopment plans are being shaped completely by each community, rather than being introduced by outside entities. The master plans for each site have incorporated the concerns and wishes of the Local Action Committees. Presenting a community that is organized, informed, and articulate will facilitate marketing of the sites to potential developers and companies.

Process of Selecting Communities for Involvement in Project

According to RDI, one of the key lessons learned was that the process for selecting communities should be more rigorous and competitive. In the *Mill Site Conversion Project for Oregon: Final Report*, submitted to EDA in February 1996, RDI wrote:

> [We need] to be sure there is a willing property owner and evidence of community commitment. Because it was a new program, we sometimes acted as if [the participants] were doing us a favor instead of the other way around, thus leading to [one] property owner (an eighth potential site) pulling out of the project. There also was weak participation of the Merlin community on the Miller Redwood site. For future work, RDI will solicit sites through a competitive process that involves some agreements ahead of time between property owners and the community about their involvement.

Potential for National Replicability of the Mill Site Conversion Project

The Mill Site Conversion Project likely will yield conclusions that can help standardize assessment/cleanup procedures for other communities facing mill closures. Of particular importance will be the generic remedies created for standard pollutants (such as hydrocarbons) commonly found at mill sites. "If this project is successful," RDI writes, "it can be used as a template for abandoned lumber or wood product mill sites throughout the Northwest and the nation."

Contacts

Lynn Youngbar
Director
Rural Development Initiatives
(541) 937-8344

Dana Peck
Project Manager
Rural Development Initiatives
(503) 236-3516

SOUTHWEST HARBOR PROJECT
Seattle, Washington

Key Players

- Port of Seattle — municipal port district; project developer and owner.
- Washington Department of Ecology — state regulatory agency, responsible for oversight of contaminated soils and sediments; joint lead agency for Environmental Impact Statement (EIS).
- U.S. Army Corps of Engineers — federal agency overseeing wetlands issues, port dredging activities, and in-water construction; joint lead agency for EIS.
- American President Lines, Ltd. — operates the new terminal owned by the Port of Seattle.
- U.S. Environmental Protection Agency, Region 10 — federal agency overseeing environmental remediation activities.
- City of Seattle — responsible for land use and building permit authorizations.

Background and Nature of the Problem

The Duwamish Corridor, Seattle's 5,300-acre industrial sector, has formed the backbone of the region's economy for over a century. Located along the eastern shore of Puget Sound, the Duwamish contains hundreds of industries, most notably the Boeing Corporation, and supports nearly 80,000 jobs that yield an annual payroll of $2.5 billion. In spite of these statistics, much of the Duwamish Corridor has experienced economic decline in recent years. One major land holder, the Port of Seattle (which owns and operates approximately 945 acres of marine cargo facilities), has sought to counter this decline by using former industrial properties to accommodate new marine terminal expansions.

One expansion project — now referred to as the Southwest Harbor Project — took shape in 1993 when an Oakland-based steamship company, American President Lines Ltd. (APL), asked the Port of Seattle to compete with other West Coast ports in an effort to accommodate APL's expanding container cargo shipment needs. The task involved developing a combined marine cargo terminal and intermodal rail yard to handle APL's increasing Pacific Rim trade.

Upon completion, this facility would be one the largest of its kind in the western United States. To meet APL's needs, the new terminal would need to be in full operation within four years, by 1997. Seattle Port officials were anxious to keep APL's existing 1,500 jobs in the Seattle area and to create 1,500 new jobs through the expansion. The project would mean huge growth for the local economy. It also would provide the catalyst for remediating idle, industrial properties that might otherwise remain contaminated.

APL officials were particularly keen on the Southwest Harbor site because they already had operations established on 83 acres of the property, which could be expanded. The site also had numerous advantages, including existing rail lines, freeways within two blocks, an international airport 15 miles away, and existing sewage and water systems. But significant challenges needed to be addressed before the deal could move forward. For example, port officials had investigated properties adjacent to APL's existing terminal, but many were in current business use. There was a strong likelihood that these properties, which had housed a wide range of industrial activities over the years, possessed widespread environmental contamination. Remediation costs potentially could exceed the market value of some properties, and the port also could face the specter of ongoing liability. Finally, the logistics of complying with all applicable federal and state regulations would be daunting, particularly since site assessment, remediation, and construction activities would occur simultaneously in order to meet APL's 1997 deadline.

Meeting the Challenge

In April 1993, port officials sat down and began negotiating with the current owners of the land surrounding APL's terminal. To their surprise, they found that most property owners were willing to negotiate detailed purchase/indemnity agreements, obviating the need to condemn the sites through eminent domain. The port's plan was to purchase approximately 145 acres, assess environmental conditions, initiate cleanup actions tailored towards future terminal needs, and ultimately lease the remediated site and completed facility to APL. It would require unprecedented cooperation between federal, state, and local agencies; participating industries; and local community members. But port officials, noting the potential long-term economic benefits, were determined to make it work.

Aerial view of Southwest Harbor Project: APL's new marine cargo terminal.

The Port of Seattle conducted remedial investigations and lengthy negotiations with current land owners to determine fair market values for the properties. "Some were tiny property owners who had no existing site information," notes Elizabeth Stetz, environmental management specialist with the Port of Seattle. "They said, 'if you want my land, you'll have to take it and assume liability for whatever's found there.'" The port agreed to this. However, for some of the larger properties, where clear and documented site contamination existed, the purchase price was negotiated in light of anticipated cleanup costs. Often negotiations were held with multiple prior owners, due to standing agreements on liability for past contamination. In these cases, the property owners placed part of the purchase price into an escrow account that was earmarked for future cleanup activities. Because these entities were paying portions of the remediation bill, they played a major role in the cleanup process, (e.g., reviewing all investigation and remedial design documents, and participating with the port in interactions with the regulatory agencies in order to ensure that their interests were protected).

The port's largest acquisition challenge was a 25-acre parcel owned by Pacific Sound Resources, a wood preserving facility that was scheduled for federal Superfund designation. The port was not interested in acquiring the property, despite its strategic location, if it meant becoming a potentially responsible party (PRP) under Superfund in the process. As the site neared listing on the National Priorities List, and the operating company's financial situation deteriorated, U.S. Environmental Protection Agency (EPA) officials realized that steep costs for site remediation would have to be borne by the Hazardous Substances Fund, known as the "Superfund" (a pool of money generated through taxes on certain chemical and petroleum companies). Facing the prospect of a $60-million cleanup, EPA allowed the property to be transferred from Pacific Sound Resources to an environmental trust, then finally to the port. EPA agreed to issue the port a Covenant-Not-to-Sue for prior environmental conditions at the site; the port, in turn, agreed to perform $21 million worth of assessment, demolition, and site remediation (including capital investment and in-kind services).

Aerial view of Southwest Harbor Project.

"EPA did not expect the Port of Seattle to bear the full $60 million for the Pacific Sound Resources site cleanup because we were not a PRP," explains the port's Stetz. "So whatever we brought to the table for the site was essentially a gift, not some sort of obligation that we had because of any liability. The federal Superfund will bear the remaining $39 million for cleanup at the site."

The port's $21 million, along with any remaining assets from Pacific Sound Resources, were placed in an environmental trust fund to be used for cleanup of this site and other sites left by Pacific Sound Resources. Over the course of remediation, the port would be reimbursed by the Superfund for $16.2 million of its original $21 million investment. EPA would oversee a cleanup that would be conducted in part by the port, and in part by EPA and its contractors, using environmental trust monies.

At the remaining properties being assembled for APL's terminal, the port decided to enter into purchasing negotiations while cleanup strategies and new construction plans were being designed. "We had to make some really risky assumptions about site conditions," says the port's Elizabeth Stetz. "We started remedial design almost the same day we started remedial investigation. Our position was: let's move forward expeditiously and modify the remedial design in the end if we've predicted wrong. So far, we have predicted really well." APL recognized that the port was fully committed to the Southwest Harbor terminal expansion and, although the lease would not be formally signed until August 1995, "they made it clear early on that they would be staying in Seattle," says Stetz.

Despite the project's momentum, opposition was mounting from surrounding residents concerned about potential noise (especially rail noise), increased truck traffic, glare from terminal lighting, as well as the quantity and quality of designated public use areas. The port launched an extensive public outreach/involvement campaign in order to ensure that all these concerns were addressed effectively. Included were Indian tribes, relevant agencies, citizen and environmental groups, and business representatives. The port's Environmental Impact Statement (EIS) project manager presented information at approximately 250 meetings and workshops, involving more than 75 community and interest groups and more than 18 federal, state, and local agencies. Public outreach also included a quarterly newsletter, small group meetings that focused on a variety of EIS topics, design workshops with the community, and interaction with a port-sponsored "Development Oversight Committee" comprised of neighborhood representatives.

Based on this public dialogue, the port made changes to the project design, including: installation of noise walls; increased public access to shorelines and buffers; use of innovative lighting technology to decrease glare; and establishment of an "Urban Impact Monitoring Group," which will review periodically the terminal's operating performance and hold the port accountable for its design and mitigation commitments.

Because the project dealt with both upland and aquatic contamination, as well as aquatic habitat restoration and economic redevelopment, a joint federal-state EIS was combined with a site-wide cleanup feasibility study. These were prepared under the supervision of three lead agencies: U.S. Army Corps of Engineers, Washington State Department of Ecology (DOE), and Port of Seattle. U.S. EPA, the City of Seattle, and the state's Department of Natural Resources were "cooperating agencies."

The port initiated an area-wide study to provide a scientific basis for determining what cleanup actions would most effectively mitigate the risks to human health and the environment posed by existing environmental problems. The risk analysis demonstrated that it was neither technically nor economically possible to attain pristine site restoration. Alternative cleanup levels were proposed, therefore, and cleanup remedies were selected on the basis of their ability to mitigate identifiable risks. For moderate level contamination, the port decided to consolidate and contain the contaminants on site. Soils that were significantly contaminated were excavated and treated. "We also provided for long-term risk management at the site," says the port's Stetz. "That means we instituted engineering and institutional controls for any remaining contamination, such as capping, maintenance procedures, and employee education." The port worked in partnership with the DOE to allow use of the "Area of Contamination" policy for the entire project area. This allowed movement of soils for remedial action without triggering state regulation for dangerous waste handling. According to port officials, avoiding those standards for on-site transport and handling saved millions of dollars.

The port spent $1.2 million evaluating sediment quality for ship berth and navigational dredging. Using advanced techniques, such as modeling of confined sediment disposal, the port was able to outline sediment cleanup alternatives for future navigational improvements at the Southwest Harbor Project, taking into consideration additional sediment cleanup actions being contemplated by state and federal agencies. The project includes plans for a submerged nearshore facility, which will provide a multi-source contaminated sediment disposal site and approximately 19 acres of clean subtidal and intertidal habitat area (a 60 percent increase of this type of habitat in Seattle's Elliott Bay).

As of summer 1996, all buildings and former structures had been demolished and most remediation was completed on the Southwest Harbor site. Port officials expect that APL's new terminal facility will be completed by October 1997.

Regulatory Framework

The cleanups have been conducted with oversight from local, state, and federal regulators, largely under orders or decrees. The wood treating facility is a federal Superfund site, and the cleanup has been conducted in part by the Port of Seattle for U.S. EPA under an Administrative Order of Consent. Certain other sites, including a shipyard, municipal landfill, and slag and scrap-steel site, are being remediated under Washington State's Superfund Program, established by the Model Toxics Control Act (MTCA). Several of the smaller properties are being addressed as "Independent Actions" under MTCA. An Independent Action involves a site cleanup that is conducted with little or no state oversight — the way 85 percent of sites in Washington are remediated. Voluntary cleanup is encouraged in Washington to promote routine and expeditious cleanup of lower-priority sites.

Financing

In Washington State, port authorities typically play a major role in the local economic development process. To finance this project, the Port of Seattle floated over $200 million in serial bonds. The interest rate for serial bonds, unlike term bonds, varies according to the year in which the bonds mature. The first $50 million, used to finance property acquisition, consisted of revenue bonds backed by the port; these bonds will mature between 1998 (at 4 percent) and 2019 (at 5.45 percent). The second $155 million, used to construct the terminal facility, was raised through general obligation bonds backed by King County taxpayers; these bonds mature over a period from 1995 (at 3.5 percent) to 2014 (at 5.34 percent). "It was critical that the port could issue bonds," says the port's Elizabeth Stetz. "We didn't have to deal with lenders having comfort with the properties, and I think that's one of the reasons why this project went through."

Impacts

A strong community action group has formed in the Duwamish Corridor to identify redevelopment initiatives for the 5,300-acre area. The group, called the Duwamish Coalition, grapples with common brownfield redevelopment issues — namely, that old industrial properties are at a competitive disadvantage, compared with urban greenfields, in terms of attracting new business. In the Duwamish Corridor, the major contaminant of concern — and thus, the main barrier to redevelopment — is total petroleum hydrocarbons (TPH). In an effort to tackle the TPH problem, coalition members teamed up with the DOE to overhaul the state's TPH regulations, incorporating a new risk-based approach. U.S. EPA awarded the Duwamish Coalition a $150,000 Brownfield Pilot Site grant in support of this regulatory effort; local governments raised an additional $100,000. The pilot project also will receive technical assistance from private-sector companies, research institutions, and various government agencies.

In searching for solutions to their brownfields problem, members of the Duwamish Coalition have carefully observed the Southwest Harbor project, noting, in particular, the risk-based remediation approach employed by the port. Based on the success of this approach, the coalition plans to enact a similar protocol to restore and revitalize properties throughout the Duwamish Corridor.

Four years into the project, the port can point to many significant achievements: timely acquisition of more than 145 acres of contaminated industrial property (when combined with existing port properties, the project area will total 180 acres), facility design for the container terminal and intermodal rail yard, and substantial cleanup of industrial property.

Lessons Learned

According to participants involved with this project, the Southwest Harbor redevelopment was facilitated by the following:

Strong Interagency Cooperation

Interagency cooperation streamlined the administrative process and reduced the costs associated with preparing an EIS and related technical studies. The President's Council on Sustainable Development cites this approach as a "national model" for environmental impact analysis. The U.S. Council on Environmental Quality praised the EIS agency team as an example of economic development combined with environmental restoration. The EIS team also was recognized by the American Society for Public Administration, receiving a public service "singular achievement" award.

Creative Project Management

Within the port, project management was facilitated by a new team concept, in which project-dedicated staff members were grouped under one manager. This team worked out of one office location and included members of the port's marine facilities, as well as staff from the legal, engineering, environmental, and finance departments.

Extensive Public Participation

The port's thorough and consistent public outreach/public involvement plan assured active participation by a wide variety of citizens in the early stages of project planning and design, helping to ensure that the project would meet port, community, and interest-group goals.

Consideration of Future Land Use

Cleanups were risk-based and tailored to meet the site's future use. The port worked with the DOE to derive site-specific soil remediation levels, which were protective of human health and the environment given future land use. Some soils have required on-site treatment based on standard state cleanup levels. After treatment, most of these soils will remain at the site and thus will be subject to institutional controls (e.g., deed restrictions). Because the port is retaining ownership of the APL property, officials can guarantee that the land remains in industrial use and that institutional controls are maintained. The Port of Seattle also used the Superfund Accelerated Cleanup Model, which incorporates concepts of presumptive remedies (preferred remedial technologies for common types of sites) and expedited actions, thereby saving both time and money.

Contacts

Elizabeth Stetz
Environmental Management Specialist
Port of Seattle
(206) 728-3191

SACRAMENTO FEDERAL COURTHOUSE (Southern Pacific Rail Yard) Sacramento, California

Key Players

- City of Sacramento — local government overseeing project.
- California Environmental Protection Agency's Department of Toxic Substances and Control — state environmental agency.
- Southern Pacific Transportation Co. (now Union Pacific) — owns 244 acres of rail yard property in downtown Sacramento; working with the city and state to remediate and redevelop the site.
- U.S. Government Services Administration — federal developer of courthouse site.
- Environmental Oversight Authority — a private consultant, acting as third-party oversight entity.

Background and Nature of Problem

The Sacramento Rail Yard, owned by the Southern Pacific Transportation Company (SPTCo), was one of central California's largest locomotive maintenance yards for nearly a century. Situated in the heart of downtown Sacramento, the 244-acre site supported a wide range of activities, including foundry and machine work, blacksmithing, painting, and cleaning. At its peak after World War II, the rail yard employed over 3,000 people. The facility has grown increasingly obsolete in recent decades, however, as SPTCo has shifted its base of operations to other locations. By fall 1996, only 100 employees remained at the site.

SPTCo's downsizing at the Sacramento rail yard gained momentum during the 1980s, at a time when the company began to investigate environmental conditions at the site. Under supervision of the California Environmental Protection Agency's Department of Toxic Substances and Control (DTSC), SPTCo conducted a series of site assessments that revealed contamination in both the soils and underlying groundwater. The facility was officially named a California Superfund site in 1988, at which time DTSC and SPTCo entered into a formal Enforceable Agreement for cleanup. The

Enforceable Agreement spelled out SPTCO's remedial duties and established a schedule for compliance. The primary contaminants of concern were heavy metals (lead), petroleum hydrocarbons (fuels and lubricants), and semivolatile organic compounds and volatile organic compounds (solvents).

The rail yard presented a challenge for DTSC officials in terms of establishing appropriate cleanup standards. The department historically had required cleanup to the most conservative "residential" level (i.e., soil that was safe enough for a child to ingest), even if a site's future use was to be commercial or industrial. This policy conformed with the National Contingency Plan — the regulation that outlines procedures to be followed in response to hazardous substance releases — which gave priority to remedial actions that were "permanent" in nature. At the Sacramento rail yard, SPTCo officials were proposing a mixed future use of commercial, residential, and recreational activities. They argued to DTSC officials that meeting a stringent residential standard on the entire 244-acre rail yard site was unnecessary and prohibitively expensive. According to Steve Hebert, vice president of Southern Pacific Real Estate Enterprises, "Initially, the state's approach was: 'we don't know what the future land use at the rail yard will be. Therefore, you must clean it up to the standard for single-family residential detached homes.' They were playing it safe, always assuming the most conservative scenario."

In the late 1980s, however, policymakers at both the national and state level began to realize that permanent solutions were not always viable. "We were spending more money than was needed to sufficiently protect public health," says DTSC's Fran Anderson. "So there was a movement toward factoring in land use and introducing institutional controls, namely deed restrictions, to complete a remedy at a site." This was precisely the approach that DTSC assumed at the rail yard: cleanup would be tailored to the site's future use, and, where contaminants were left in place, deed restrictions would be placed on the property to ensure that only appropriate uses occurred.

Soon after the Enforceable Agreement was signed in 1988, Rio Grande Industries, a Colorado-based rail company, acquired SPTCo (the corporate name "Southern Pacific Transportation Company" was retained). This acquisition signaled the end of the Sacramento Rail Yard's days. "There was a shift toward cutting out inefficiencies and centralizing operations," says SPTCo's Hebert. "The Sacramento buildings were old, the equipment there was old, and it was just cheaper to build new facilities elsewhere."

With operations phasing out and remediation underway, SPTCo officials began to contemplate reuse options for the site. They could either sell the property or hold and redevelop it themselves. "There was a considerable amount of debt that needed to be retired," says SPTCo's Hebert. "We looked at the assets in Southern Pacific's real estate portfolio and decided that staying with the Sacramento rail yard property was a smart idea. The potential for reuse was intriguing enough that we decided to [keep the site and] take it through the redevelopment process."

Meeting the Challenge

Officials from SPTCo, the city, and DTSC were negotiating redevelopment of the rail yard in the early 1990s when a new factor emerged. The federal government announced its interested in building a new courthouse in Sacramento, preferably in a central downtown location. City officials quickly concluded that a particular two-and-a-half acre block in the heart of Sacramento was the logical place. Two-thirds of this parcel was a city-owned former vehicle maintenance yard; one-third of the block was part of SPTCo's rail yard. The plan was to join the two properties and turn them over to the U.S. Government Services Administration (GSA), the agency that owns and develops federal real estate.

From the start, SPTCo and the city both supported the idea of a federal courthouse project. "We saw the courthouse as an opportunity to kick off broader redevelopment on Southern Pacific's land," says SPTCo's Hebert. "There was potential spin-off, other real estate opportunities, from this."

More importantly, though, the courthouse would provide a test case for policies to be implemented on the remaining 240 acres of the Southern Pacific's rail yard. Key issues needed to be resolved, such as, what level of cleanup would the state require? How would the DTSC and the city coordinate their responsibilities at the site? The courthouse would be a proving ground for new policies aimed at tackling these questions.

One of the greatest challenges involved deed restrictions that had been placed on SPTCO's property following remediation during the 1980s. "DTSC had been responsible for doing formal overall site cleanup at the rail yards," says Fran Anderson, DTSC's chief of the Sacramento Responsible Parties Unit. "However, we recognized that, as we were going through site assessment and remediation, we weren't getting *all* the contamination. Some contamination, in fact, was being left in place. As a result, when we certified portions of the property as having 'completed the remedial plan,' we limited site use to industrial/commercial under a deed restriction." For the courthouse project, the properties belonging to the city and SPTCo were joined, at which time SPTCo's deed restrictions became applicable at *both* properties.

There were three types of deed restrictions on the rail yard (and courthouse) site. First, DTSC had limited site use to commercial and industrial activities, meaning that any planned residential or recreational use would have to be authorized by DTSC. Second, the deed restrictions specified that the site could never be excavated without concurrence from the DTSC. Third, the deed restrictions established that groundwater from the property could never be used for any purpose.

In terms of redeveloping the rail yard site, these deed restrictions were a double-edged sword. On the one hand, they guaranteed involvement by the state environmental agency and, therefore, ensured protection of public health. On the other hand, they created a strong disincentive for redevelopment by introducing the probability of significant time delays — a red flag for any developer. "The bottom line is that developers are worried about costs and time frames," explains DTSC's Fran Anderson. "But DTSC is a state agency whose mission is protection of public health. When DTSC is setting priorities, we first address things that are presenting a significant endangerment to public health and the environment. We often can't get to the lower-priority work, such as reviewing deed restrictions for land use or authorizing changes at remediated sites, as quickly as developers might like. We just have limited staff to work on all these problems."

Wendy Saunders, senior management analyst with the City of Sacramento, agrees that DTSC would have been overwhelmed at the rail yard facility. "The plan for the entire rail yard site calls for ten million square feet of office space, 2,800 housing units, and nearly 30 acres of parks — no small development," she says. "Under the deed restriction, DTSC would have needed to review literally every development permit application, which would have been an extraordinary amount of work. DTSC is not even remotely set up — in terms of staffing levels or expertise — to undertake this task. Furthermore, it would have introduced an aspect of uncertainty into the Southern Pacific property; the deed restriction says only that DTSC approval of excavation is required, not *what it takes* to get that approval."

In response to this deed restriction problem, the key parties involved with the courthouse — SPTCo, the city, and DTSC — teamed together and crafted an innovative solution. They signed a Memorandum of Understanding (MOU) in December 1994 that outlined specific roles, responsibilities, and procedures for the courthouse project. The most significant aspect of the MOU was that the state and city both agreed to relinquish some of their oversight responsibilities to a third-party oversight entity, known as the Environmental Oversight Authority (EOA). The EOA would be, according to the city's Wendy Saunders, "the eyes and ears for *both* the state and city." The MOU reads:

> Rather than require both Department and City review and approval of every application for development in the rail yards, to promote efficient and orderly development of the site the Parties have developed a program, to be jointly administered by the City and [DTSC], that will allow efficient development and meet the protective goals of the deed restrictions.

The EOA was tasked with overseeing most on-site activities at the courthouse, including excavation, handling, disposal of, and exposure to potentially contaminated soils and groundwater. To ensure that all activities were conducted according to DTSC and city requirements, the City of Sacramento wrote a detailed "Field Procedures Manual" for the EOA. Finished in 1994, the draft manual outlines standard procedures for the entire 244-acre rail yard, including how to: (a) recognize and deal with contamination; (b) characterize the nature and extent of contamination; and (c) verify that contamination has been adequately remediated at the site. "Basically, we used the courthouse site as a pilot project, a way to do beta-testing on the manuals," says DTSC's Anderson. "The experience helped us determine where the bugs were and what needed to be clarified." The final draft of the Field Procedures Manual is due to be completed by winter 1997.

From the outset, SPTCo had focused on ensuring community involvement with rail yard redevelopment. In the early 1990s, the company and the City of Sacramento had conducted a series of focus group meetings for neighborhood organizers, local businesses, neighborhood representatives, and environmental groups. SPTCo encountered overwhelming public support for the project, particularly from environmental groups who opposed the sprawling development that was fast consuming pristine agricultural lands around Sacramento. "This was a time when the city and county had been going through a contentious land development period," says SPTCo's Hebert. "There was disagreement about whether urban sprawl should be supported or stopped, all [of which] caused a great deal of fighting and controversy. We came in the door at this time, which was fortunate. Our proposed project was in the city core, near existing light rail and highways, close to existing infrastructure — everything that all these environmental groups said they wanted, namely, urban infill rather than suburban expansion."

Aerial view of Southern Pacific's 244-acre railyard prior to redevelopment.

Artist's rendering of redeveloped Sacramento rail yard area.

In March 1994, the city and SPTCo assembled their properties and transferred them over to GSA which placed $2.5 million into an escrow account — money that was earmarked for improvements in local utilities and streets. As part of the land transfer, SPTCo and the city both agreed to retain liability for additional environmental contamination discovered on their separate properties during excavation and construction.

That same year, the city selected a local engineering firm, Helmick & Lerner Inc., to be the Environmental Oversight Authority for the courthouse site. Construction began several months later. Contractors excavated nearly 30 feet of soil to make room for the building's foundation. The primary contaminants found during this process were petroleum hydrocarbons (containing volatile organic compounds and polycyclic aromatic hydrocarbons), lead, benzene, ethyl benzene, and chloroform. The EOA observed excavation activities once every three hours; for soil handling activities, the EOA made an observation during the handling of each aggregate 1,000 cubic yards.

In establishing cleanup levels, DTSC drew on the same protocol used for the broader rail yard site. Remediation would not be conducted to background (pristine) levels, but rather, acceptable levels of chemicals could be left in place, depending on the potential for human exposure to soils. For areas where exposure likely would be (e.g., parks and all open spaces, including landscaped strips), the city and DTSC required that clean fill be imported from off-site. For areas beneath industrial or commercial buildings, such as the courthouse, soils had to be remediated to a less stringent standard (although clean enough for construction workers to be protected from unacceptable exposure).

DTSC issued a Letter of Completion to the city in June 1996, stating that the city's portion of the courthouse site was cleaned up according to commercial standards. By September 1996, excavation was complete and the exterior framework of the courthouse was in place. The GSA's Gilbert Delgado estimates that the building will be operational by 1998.

"Lots of issues surfaced during the courthouse construction," says the city's Wendy Saunders. Plenty of contamination [was discovered], more construction de-watering occurred than was planned for, and some of the rules for handling and disposing of soils were violated. But it was a real learning experience from which we all [benefitted]." In total, the city spent nearly $500,000 on remediation for its portion of the property. "We discovered plenty of contamination [on the city's land] that was not anticipated," says the city's

Saunders. By contrast, Southern Pacific spent under $10,000 for remediation on its portion of the courthouse site.

With the courthouse well underway, SPTCo and the city have focused their attention on redeveloping the remaining 240 acres of the Sacramento Rail Yard. The current plan calls for mixed commercial/residential/recreational uses. SPTCo expects to develop various sites and then sell them to interested buyers. "Soon we'll have the zoning in place for them to move forward," says the city's Saunders. The draft zoning ordinance establishes the following requirements to ensure compliance with DTSC deed restrictions:

- proposed land use must match implemented cleanup levels;
- enough confirmation sampling must be done on a given parcel to assure that construction worker health and safety is protected;
- adequate construction worker health and safety plans must be in place;
- any construction de-watering that occurs must not exacerbate groundwater problems or pose public health threats;
- construction will occur under the purview of the Environmental Oversight Authority, which will make certain that any contamination uncovered during the course of excavation is appropriately addressed;
- clean fill must be placed in all landscaped and open space areas.

Regulatory Framework

Two-thirds of the courthouse property originally was owned by the City of Sacramento, and one-third by SPTCo. The SPTCo portion, a state Superfund site, had been cleaned up pursuant to a 1988 Enforceable Agreement between DTSC and Southern Pacific. When the site cleanup was certified as complete, DTSC recognized that certain contaminants remained on site. As such, a deed restriction was placed on the property, which stipulated the following: (1) only industrial/commercial uses could occur at the property; (2) any excavation would require DTSC oversight; and (3) the groundwater could not be used for any reason.

Unlike SPTCo's portion of the courthouse property, the city's portion had not been remediated prior to the 1990s. The city's parcel was enrolled in California's Voluntary Cleanup Program (VCP), which is administered by the California Department of Toxic Substances Control (DTSC). The VCP is designed for voluntary cleanups at sites having relatively simple contamination. More com-plex sites will be considered for the program if DTSC feels that the project has strong redevelopment potential — as was the case for the Sacramento rail yard facility.

Under the VCP, DTSC's services are administered through a negotiated contract, called a Voluntary Cleanup Agreement (VCA), which is not an enforcement order. In June 1994, DTSC entered into a VCA with the city for its portion of courthouse property. The agreement spelled out what was required of the city in terms of site assessment and cleanup, and established a time line for completion. Two years later, in 1996, when remediation at the courthouse site was finished, DTSC issued the city a letter of completion. The letter reduces, but does not completely eliminate, the city's liability. DTSC has billed the city $40,000 for oversight costs to date.

Financing

The city spent $500,000 on site assessment and remediation at its portion of the courthouse property; SPTCo spent only $10,000. In 1995, the City of Sacramento applied for, and received, a $200,000 Brownfields Pilot Site grant from the U.S. Environmental Protection Agency (EPA). The grant money was targeted towards development of the environmental oversight program and implementation of the Environmental Oversight Authority. "When we started the courthouse project, it was really a test case to see how the environmental oversight program would work," says the city's Wendy Saunders. To date, the city has spent $50,000 on the Environmental Oversight Authority.

Impacts

The courthouse is a $142-million, 380,000-square-foot facility that will produce more than 1,000 new construction jobs and 200 permanent jobs. It is the single biggest construction project in the city's history. "The courthouse sits on the southern boundary of the Southern Pacific site," says the city's Saunders, "and we hope it becomes the gateway to the rest of the rail yard development."

Lessons Learned

According to participants involved with this project, redevelopment of the Sacramento rail yard was facilitated by the following:

Strong Public/Private Cooperation

All parties involved with the courthouse development agree that public/private cooperation was the cornerstone of the project's success. "Everyone was interested in making this project work," says the city's Wendy Saunders. "DTSC was involved and helpful when decisions needed to be made. Southern Pacific was also incredibly helpful." DTSC's Fran Anderson adds, "It was encouraging to bring different parties together and have everyone focus on finding solutions rather than simply establishing positions."

This project was not without communication snags, however. "We learned that the requirements of the Environmental Oversight Authority program need to be very clearly communicated to all affected parties," says the city's Saunders. "It does no good if the program is understood at the top but not clear to the contractors and sub-contractors who actually do the work. In refining the Environmental Oversight Program for use on the remainder of the rail yard, we will make sure that this heightened communication happens."

The Memorandum of Understanding (MOU)

The MOU is this project's most important and innovative aspect because it has helped overcome a major barrier: the challenge of coping with the site's deed restrictions. To address these barriers, the MOU established a third-party Environmental Oversight Authority (EOA) to be administered by the City of Sacramento. "The MOU was a system of checks and balances," says DTSC's Anderson. "It helped establish a plan of action for three groups with very different missions. DTSC's primary concern is cleanup and remediation, the city's primary concern is land use, and the developer and landowner are focused on keeping costs down. The MOU brought all these [disparate] groups together."

"I think that everyone involved understood that the Environmental Oversight Authority (EOA) had authority," says Gilbert Delgado, architect and project manager for the GSA. "We felt that the EOA spoke for the city and state and we abided by what it said. It worked very well." Steve Hebert with SPTCO agrees, "The MOU was important because it established some clear roles and responsibilities between the three parties, which is especially meaningful given how far apart we all were at different points in the process."

The MOU also will provide a level of "comfort" for future buyers and lenders of the redeveloped parcels. "When we go out to market the property," says SPTCo's Hebert, "it will be clear to land purchasers and investors who has been responsible for what. There's some certainty in place that wasn't there before the MOU." The city's Saunders agrees that the MOU has streamlined the process. "[The MOU has allowed us to] set up one-stop shopping," she says. "This means that you don't have to go to DTSC if you want to excavate [on the rail yard site], you just need to come to the city. We'll take care of all the regulatory agency's concerns."

Strong Market Conditions and Location

"This project worked because there was a land owner that had an incentive to proceed," says SPTCO's Steve Hebert. "In other words, there was an opportunity for redevelopment and, therefore, an opportunity to recover some of our remediation costs. Negotiations would have been very different if the market conditions had not been as strong as they were."

Cleanup Standards That Were Tailored to the Site's End Use

In the 1980s, DTSC officials began to realize that requiring cleanup at contaminated sites to the most conservative or "residential" levels was not always necessary, particularly if the site was slated to support industrial or commercial use in the future. At the Sacramento rail yard, the department decided to let SPTCo tailor site cleanup to its intended end use — a mixture of commercial, residential, and recreational activities. Without this shift in policy towards land-based cleanup standards, cleanup of the rail yard would have taken substantially longer and been exorbitantly expensive. Indeed, SPTCo might have simply conducted the necessary remediation and then "mothballed" the facility (i.e., put up a fence, posted No Trespassing signs, and left the property vacant). SPTCo's Steve Hebert explains why he thinks DTSC was willing to allow tailored cleanup standards. "In the early 1980s, if SPTCo had gone to the state and simply said, 'we want to do a land-based cleanup,' I don't think DTSC would have gone for it," Hebert says. "But because SPTCo and the city went together with *an approved land use plan* in hand, DTSC was willing to agree to it. The land use plan was critical — it meant we didn't have to *wonder* what the end use for the property would be, and it showed that we had community support for our ideas."

Opportunity to Shape Policies for the Rest of Rail Yard Site

"The courthouse was a proving ground for policies and procedures that would be implemented for the larger Southern Pacific redevelopment area," says DTSC's Fran Anderson. Based on experiences at the courthouse site, the Field Procedures Manual (the book that detailed procedures for site investigation and handling of contaminated materials) was amended for use during redevelopment of the remaining 240 acres of rail yard. "If the courthouse project hadn't come along, the MOU might have looked very different," says SPTCO's Hebert. "The courthouse gave us a 'test case' for developing long-term policies at the rest of the Southern Pacific site."

Contacts

Wendy Saunders
Senior Management Analyst
City Manager's Office
City of Sacramento
(916) 264-8196

Mark Melani
Project Manager
Southern Pacific Rail Yard Site
Department of Toxic Substances and Control (DTSC)
(916) 255-3606

Steve Hebert, Vice President
Southern Pacific Real Estate Enterprises
(303) 812-7614

ROSS'S LANDING AND THE TENNESSEE AQUARIUM
Chattanooga, Tennessee

Key Players

- RiverValley Partners — local public/private development group.
- The Lyndhurst Foundation — Chattanooga-based foundation providing backing for the project.

Background and Nature of Problem

Two hundred years ago, Cherokee chieftain John Ross established a prominent trading post along the banks of the Tennessee River, nestled in the Cumberland Mountains. This trading center, known as Ross's Landing, grew steadily over the years, serving as a prime hub for river and railroad transport for the southeastern United States. The center expanded into a bustling city, later taking on the name Chattanooga. In the late 1800s, the industrial revolution swept Chattanooga, and factories and warehouses appeared all along the riverfront. The city became a powerhouse of industrial activity, fueled by the large coal deposits on nearby Cumberland Plateau. For many years, the local Chamber of Commerce boasted that "Chattanooga had the greatest diversity of manufacturing in America!" By the late 1960s, however, it was clear that Chattanooga had paid a high price for this prosperity. "We were chosen by the U.S. Department of Health, Education, and Welfare as having the dirtiest air in America," says Jim Bowen, vice president of RiverValley Partners, a local public/private development group. "And that was scary — it felt like a young man having a heart attack."

Chattanooga buckled down and began tackling its environmental problems in the 1970s, at a time when the city's strong industrial economy was shifting to a more service-oriented base. Businesses began moving inland, away from the river, leaving behind abandoned factories and uncertain site contamination scenarios along the waterfront. Many of the city's waterways, it turned out, were choked with industrial sludge and waste. Chattanooga Creek, which runs through a predominantly low-income minority neighborhood, was determined by U.S. Environmental Protection Agency

(EPA) to be one of the most polluted streams in the country — yet another designation that pummeled the city's self-image. Officials recall a climate at that time characterized by economic recession, heightened social tension, and general urban decline.

Meeting the Challenge

As Chattanooga officials in the 1980s searched for ways to link environmental remediation with economic revitalization, they identified cleanup and redevelopment of the waterfront as a top priority and established a task force to investigate reuse alternatives. Public interest in the initiative was overwhelming, with thousands of Chattanoogans attending hundreds of meetings between 1982 and 1985. What emerged was a community vision to "rediscover the Tennessee River — the asset we had forgotten," says RiverValley Partners' Bowen. Residents felt that Chattanooga's revitalization should emanate from the historic, waterfront area called Ross's Landing. "We had turned our back on the river," says Bowen. "But now we began to envision the river as a necklace — one that would have little gems and pearls along the way, with development at Ross's Landing being the crown jewel."

The task force published a 20-year Tennessee Riverpark Master Plan that called for "a continuous circuit of parks, trails, and landmarks...that would be a catalyst for new development that included new industry, retail, office space, and housing. It [also] would generate new permanent jobs and increased tax revenues." The task force set forth three guiding principles for the community:

- ***build*** on Chattanooga's assets: natural beauty, fascinating history, and industry;
- ***preserve*** and enhance these natural and historic treasures, carefully adding private development sites along the river; and
- ***create*** new parks, trails, attractions, and industry to replace run-down and abandoned spaces.

During these years, a parallel community planning effort was underway called Vision 2000. Addressing a broader scope than riverfront revitalization alone, Vision 2000 was the incubator for innovative programs on energy-efficiency, sustainable development, social justice, and neighborhood improvement. Launched in 1984, this comprehensive process also brought together thousands of local residents who discussed ideas, voiced concerns, and plotted a course for the city's future. The result was publication of the community's "Commitment Portfolio," a compendium of 40 goals articulating a new sense of public spirit and determination. Vision 2000 was one of the first and most comprehensive community-wide goal setting initiatives in the country. The objectives of these two planning efforts — the task force's Tennessee Riverpark Master Plan and the broader Vision 2000 process — strongly complemented one another. Both groups envisioned that the cornerstones to Chattanooga's redevelopment were: 1) construction of the public access area known as Ross's Landing; and 2) construction of the nation's first freshwater aquarium, the Tennessee Aquarium.

To oversee the implementation and financing of these projects, the Riverpark Master Plan called for establishment of the RiverCity Company, a privately-funded, non-profit corporation. Between 1987 and 1990, RiverCity Company (now RiverValley Partners), purchased almost ten acres of property along the waterfront from various owners for $4.5 million. Four of these ten acres were eventually donated to the City of Chattanooga and Hamilton County for construction of Ross's Landing and the Tennessee Aquarium; the remaining six acres were retained by RiverValley for private development later on. Subsequently, the City of Chattanooga sold the adjoining 13-acre former Kirkman High School campus to RiverValley for $3.5 million. This site now includes the Creative Discovery Museum (children's museum), a Marriott Residence Inn, and the new 3-D IMAX Theater recently opened by the Tennessee Aquarium.

The Riverpark Master Plan called for an estimated $750 million in investment — a formidable task given Chattanooga's cash-strapped status. Analysts estimated that the first $150 million would need to be raised through the public sector; the remaining $600 million hopefully would come from the private sector coordinated by the RiverCity Company. Fortunately, eight local foundations and seven financial institutions donated $12 million in non-restrictive grant funds to capitalize the RiverCity Company. The money was placed in a revolving fund — to assemble land, create plans, and serve as a catalyst for public/private investment.

The key player was the Lyndhurst Foundation, built on the fortune of the Lupton family, the first bottlers of Coca Cola in the United States in 1899. Bruz Clark, vice president of the Lyndhurst Foundation, says, "There was a sense that Chattanooga had a lot going for it, but morale was low and some major employers had pulled out of town. The feeling at the Foundation was that we had major assets and could help turn things around, but first we needed a strong vision." The Lyndhurst Foundation, in fact, made the Vision 2000 process a reality by pouring in over $200,000 to the effort.

After the RiverValley Partners had purchased ten waterfront acres, it moved forward with Phase I and Phase II environmental assessments. "There were some unknowns," notes RiverValley Partners' Bowen, "but we were fairly certain that there were no serious environmental problems because previous activities at the site included light industry and warehousing, not heavy industry." Fortunately, their gamble panned out. The only discoveries included a few minor underground storage tanks, subsequently removed under state supervision. "Once we had environmental clearance, it was easy sledding from there on out," Bowen concludes. The group then applied for building permits, required by the U.S. Army Corps of Engineers and the Tennessee Valley Authority (TVA), for construction along the river corridor. In 1989, construction began on the Tennessee Aquarium.

One year later, construction began for Ross's Landing, the four-acre park and pedestrian plaza that serves as the setting for the Tennessee Aquarium. It features a raised and planted entry arch, waterwall, a new boat dock and rowing launch, and sitting and dining areas throughout the plaza. The land was donated to the city by RiverCity Company, but all project costs — totaling $10 million for design, construction, infrastructure improvements, and road relocation — were financed by the public. By May 1992, both the Tennessee Aquarium and Ross's Landing were open to the public.

The Aquarium is the only museum dedicated to freshwater ecosystems in the United States. It is the largest of its kind in the world. According to its brochures, the facility offers visitors an in-depth look at the Tennessee River ecosystem from its headwaters in the Appalachian highlands, to its eventual conclusion in the Gulf of Mexico. Many exhibits allow observers to actually stroll through terrariums, being completely surrounded with a diversity of freshwater flora and fauna. The unique aspect of the Aquarium project is that it was designed and built with private funds. Individuals, corporations, foundation, and organizations donated over $45 million to the effort; when the Aquarium opened its doors in May 1992, it was completely debt-free. RiverValley Partners notes that in its first year, the Aquarium drew nearly 1.5 million visitors — more than double the projected number. These numbers have remained relatively stable in the years since. "What was once abandoned manufacturing and warehouse space is now a tremendous economic generator for Chattanooga," boasts literature from RiverValley Partners. "Since its opening, the Aquarium has served as a beacon for Chattanooga's riverfront development and the renaissance of the downtown area."

With waterfront redevelopment well underway, officials began in the mid-1990s to turn their attention inland towards the rest of Chattanooga, where a range of issues still persisted — environmental injustice, insufficient job training, difficulties associated with recycling old industrial lands or "brownfields," and a school system in need of help. To meet these many challenges, the RiverCity Company merged with Partners for Economic Progress, a traditional, primarily publicly-funded economic development agency, to form the new RiverValley Partners. RiverValley Partners has worked tirelessly in the past two years to tackle this mountain of social, environmental, and economic issues. What remains to be seen is whether this organization, which so expertly managed riverfront redevelopment, also can handle a much broader array of problems, in a much larger geographic area, with the same level of success.

Regulatory Framework

At the time this project was launched, Tennessee did not have a state voluntary cleanup program. All site assessment and remediation activities for Ross's Landing and the Tennessee Aquarium were conducted under the authority and supervision of the state environmental agency. Construction permits, obtained for work along the river corridor, were approved by U.S. Army Corps of Engineers and the Tennessee Valley Authority.

Financing

The property for Ross's Landing and the Tennessee Aquarium was acquired by RiverValley Partners between 1987 and 1990 with $4.5 million in private funds. The company donated four acres to the City of Chattanooga and Hamilton County for construction of the facilities, reserving the remaining six for its own development initiatives. "We kept that acreage around the fringes, with the idea being that we'd recoup our costs on this project there. And, as you might expect, land values have shot up significantly around Ross's Landing," says RiverValley Partners' Jim Bowen.

According to company officials, eight local foundations and seven financial institutions raised $12 million in non-restrictive grant funds to capitalize the RiverCity Company. The money was used as a revolving fund — to assemble land, create plans, and serve as a catalyst for public/private investment. Of the initial $12 million raised to capitalize construction of Ross's Landing and the Tennessee Aquarium, $10 million came from the local Lyndhurst Foundation. "We just felt that it was necessary — and within our capacity — to kick off the project," says Lyndhurst Foundation's vice president, Bruz Clark. The foundation continues to finance projects through RiverValley Partners, including ongoing construction of the River-park greenway and operation of the Planning and Design Center downtown.

The costs associated with Ross's Landing park and plaza — for design, construction, infrastructure improvements, and road relocation — totaled over $10 million. The land, itself, was donated to the city by the RiverValley Partners, but all remaining costs were shouldered by the public sector. Funding sources included the State of Tennessee ($7,350,000), the local hotel/motel tax ($2,500,000), and the Tennessee Wildlife Fund ($200,000). The City of Chattanooga and Hamilton County spend $2 million annually to fund the operations and maintenance for Ross's Landing park and plaza, which includes the five-mile system of riverfront parks, trails, and bridges. The $45-million Tennessee Aquarium was completely financed by private contributions from individuals, corporations, foundations, organizations; no tax money or other public funds were used for that project.

RiverValley Partners' annual budget draws from both public and private sources. It includes approximately $800,000 in public funds ($400,000 from both the city and the county) and upwards of $2 million in private funds.

Impacts

According to RiverValley Partners, the aquarium has been the catalyst for more that $793 million in investment in the Chattanooga area. The private sector is responsible for 73.8 percent of that investment, with the balance from public sources: 12.2 percent from federal grants, 6.2 percent from the City of Chattanooga, 6.2 percent from the State of Tennessee, and 1.7 percent from Hamilton County. The aquarium also has provided an important educational, research, and cultural asset to the city. Hundreds of thousands of school children have participated in the facility's educational programs. The staff biologists are earning the aquarium a reputation as an excellent freshwater study resource.

In the past 20 years, Chattanooga has undergone a radical transformation by any standards. It has emerged from being one of the most polluted cities in America in the late 1970s, to being a pioneer of environmentalism and sustainable development in the 1990s. In 1994, Partners for Livable Cities named Chattanooga one of the 17 "most livable places to live" in the United States. That same year, the city was showcased while it hosted a meeting for the President's Council on Sustainable Development. While access to the river used to be minimal, now there is a five-mile corridor of walkways and jogging paths lining the shores. In 1996, the city celebrated its 13th Annual River Bend Festival, a music event that attracts hundreds of thousands of people each year. In May 1996, officials announced that a new $12-million sports medicine complex is to be located in downtown Chattanooga.

"It's amazing to see the transformation," says the Lyndhurst Foundation's Clark. "I've seen this city at its worst, only 16 years ago, and now I'm seeing it at its best." Vice President Albert Gore echoed this sentiment in January 1995 at the President's Council on Sustainable Development meeting: "[A]ny company looking for a place to locate that is deeply committed to sustainable development and has extraordinary quality of life for men and women who work in the company — Chattanooga is the place to come."

Lessons Learned

According to participants involved with this project, redevelopment of the Chattanooga riverfront was facilitated by the following:

The Project's Waterfront Location, Which Offset Possible Environmental Risks

A common problem with many brownfield sites is that they are located in geographically undesirable locations (i.e., on the outskirts of town or in an impoverished neighborhood). Even without the threat of contamination, such sites might not be attractive to developers or lenders for pure market reasons. On the other hand, brownfields that are located in desirable locations (i.e., near a downtown core or along a waterfront) stand a better chance of being redeveloped, especially if potential financial gains from the project outweigh the costs of addressing environmental contamination. RiverValley Partners took this risk when it acquired property along the waterfront for development of the Tennessee Aquarium and Ross's Landing, and, fortunately, major contamination was not discovered.

Strong "Community Vision" for Growth

The Tennessee Riverpark Master Plan was the result of a three-year, comprehensive, community-wide visioning process that brought together thousands of Chattanooga residents. This effort was augmented by the city-wide redevelopment initiative, Vision 2000. The Lyndhurst Foundation's Clark says of Vision 2000, "It was truly a community process. No idea was considered absurd."

The primary source of funding for Vision 2000 was the Chattanooga-based Lyndhurst Foundation. According to RiverValley Partners, the goals set forth within Vision 2000 already have generated over $793 million in "spin off" investment, three-quarters of which came from the private sector, one-quarter of which was public investment.

Strong Public/Private Partnerships

"A lot of communities come up with ideas and visions but they don't have a group of people working a minimum of eight hours a day to get it done," says RiverValley Partners' Jim Bowen. "Local government is generally not equipped, in terms of time or staff, to handle these types of issues." The Tennessee RiverValley Master Plan, unveiled in 1985, specifically recommended that a company would be put in place to assist local governments implement the plan — hence, the birth of the RiverCity Company (later RiverValley Partners).

RiverValley Partners is a public/private non-profit organization that focuses on economic redevelopment in Chattanooga and Hamilton County. Funded largely through private sources, RiverValley aims to attract and retain companies in the city that will provide high-paying jobs in sustainable "clean" businesses. RiverValley Partners notes that its organization "focuses on creating an environment where business and industry can grow. Neither the public nor private sector can do this alone."

"RiverValley Partners has been successful because a lot of thought went into how to implement the vision," echoes Bruz Clark of the Lyndhurst Foundation. The only concern at this point, he adds, is that the group's mission may become too overwhelming as it moves away from a riverfront development focus and assumes a broader community-wide agenda.

Financial Investment From the Public and Private Sectors

Chattanooga was able to implement its ambitious redevelopment program because of strong financial support from both the public and private sectors. The city is blessed with the presence of several local foundations — most notably the Lyndhurst Foundation — that are committed to ensuring Chattanooga's economic, social, and environmental health.

Emphasis on Quality Construction During Redevelopment

Chattanoogans made a commitment to rebuilding their city with style. "Quality planning, design, and construction are required elements of a successful city," RiverValley Partners' Bowen notes. "If you skimp on quality at any of these levels, you dramatically lessen your chance of success."

Capitalizing on the Particular Strengths and Attributes of the Chattanooga Community

Chattanooga has not only a strong industrial heritage, but also a rich cultural and artistic history. Many in the city believe that capitalizing on this strong legacy — tapping into the city's historic identity — has been critical in terms of emerging from the dark years of the 1970s. Bruz Clark of the Lyndhurst Foundation notes, "We all took a hard look at what the community had to offer, we examined our roots and our heritage of the river." This reflection, he says, enabled the city to chart a strong course for future growth. The construction of Ross's Landing, in particular, held a great deal of meaning for residents of Chattanooga because it marks the original Cherokee landing point, and, as such, is a symbol of the city's birthplace.

Because there is such a strong sense of connection to the city's history, residents were eager to finance the project through both public and private avenues. "That's a quality unique to Chattanooga," notes RiverValley Partners' Bowen. "We give to the arts and charitable groups in excess of the national average, perhaps because this has always been such a heavily industrialized town with strong industrial leaders."

For Chattanooga, reconnecting the public to the river was the critical first step in the city's renaissance. "Now people are very excited," says the Lyndhurst Foundation's Clark. "There's self esteem and pride — you can feel the confidence in the air. In the

1970s and 1980s, people wanted to leave Chattanooga. Now the young people are all flocking back."

RiverValley Partners' Bowen agrees, "Chattanooga is truly on a roll now. We're in that rare period of our local history where we have had a few success stories and therefore our public and private leaders have a 'shared confidence' in each other. That has bred a degree of risk-taking among our private and public lenders heretofore missing. Now when a project comes down the pike, we give a thorough review and, if it has merit, we try to determine how to fund it. Before, we were just as likely to spend enormous time, talent, and money to figure out how not to do it."

Contacts

Jim Bowen, Vice President
RiverValley Partners
(423) 265-3700

Jack Murrah, President
or
Bruz Clark, Vice President
The Lyndhurst Foundation
(423) 756-0767

LOUISVILLE DRYER COMPANY (Ni-Chro Plating, Inc.) Louisville, Kentucky

Key Players

- City of Louisville — local government overseeing project.
- Louisville Landbank Authority — public entity that represents the taxing authorities (city, county, school board, and state) and is responsible for handling transactions and holding title to tax-foreclosed properties.
- Louisville Dryer Company (formerly Clemco Fabricator) — neighbor purchasing Ni-Chro Plating site for its business expansion.
- Kentucky Department of Environmental Protection — state oversight agency.

Background and Nature of Problem

Like many cities across America, Louisville, Kentucky, has witnessed a steady migration of jobs and economic opportunity to the suburbs — a trend that spells trouble for urban areas left behind. Louisville's commercial-industrial quarter, the West End, has been hit particularly hard by this phenomenon. City officials report that nearly a quarter of the land here is either abandoned or underutilized, and that nearly 48 percent of residents, predominantly minorities, live below the poverty line. Efforts to revitalize the area are complicated by the fact that residential homes are mixed in among industrial-zoned areas. "At the time this area was developed," says Rich Campbell, a U.S. Environmental Protection Agency (EPA) employee on a brownfields detail to the City of Louisville, "there were weak or non-existent zoning restrictions. As a result, you have a hodge-podge of land uses," many of which are incompatible with one another.

One abandoned industrial property in the West End — previously owned by Ni-Chro Plating, Inc. — housed a half-acre metal-finishing plant that began operations in 1977. In 1981, EPA notified Ni-Chro that it must register as a hazardous waste generator, but, according to EPA documents, Ni-Chro representatives told the Kentucky Division of Waste Management that they did not need to register because they were going out of business. In 1983, however, some form of business resumed in the building and operated illegally for roughly six months. Three years later, the state and the Jefferson County Health Department surveyed the site and inventoried a range of chemical substances, including cyanide stripping solutions, acids, caustics, cleaners, heavy metal brighteners, and various organic compounds. The EPA determined that this facility presented an immediate threat to human health because:

- The plant was located in a heavily populated urban area;
- Hazardous, incompatible materials were carelessly stored at the site; and
- The potential existed for the generation or accidental formation and release of toxic hydrogen cyanide gas.

In 1987, EPA proceeded with an emergency removal of contaminants at the site. Because the prior owner had vanished, EPA absorbed the $168,000 remediation cost and then placed a lien on the property for the same amount. Meanwhile, roughly $25,000 in back taxes had accumulated.

For nearly seven years, the Ni-Chro Plating site remained inactive. Then, in October 1994, a neighboring business owner named Phil Clements approached the city's Office of Economic Development with an offer. Clements was interested in purchasing the site to expand his asphalt equipment refabrication business, (then called Clemco Fabricator, but since renamed Louisville Dryer Company), provided the city resolved all environmental problems associated with the property and offered protection from future liability. At the time, Clements employed approximately 25 people; through expansion, he hoped to add at least 10-15 jobs. According to EPA's Rich Campbell, "Clements said that if he couldn't get the abandoned site, he would have to relocate somewhere else. Without the city getting involved, there was no hope of the transaction occurring."

That same year, Louisville launched a city-wide brownfields redevelopment initiative as part of its Empowerment Zone application to the U.S. Department of Housing and Urban Development (HUD). Although the city was not successful in its Empowerment Zone application, it was named an Enterprise Community (EC) and awarded $3 million. City officials emphasize that the strategic planning process of applying for the HUD grant involved an unprecedented level of community participation — more than 100 members of the Louisville community came together to shape comprehensive plans for economic revitalization.

Local experts and representatives from key institutions formed "practitioner groups" to address specific issues under the umbrella of economic revitalization. The Environmental Practitioner's Group was one such task force. "There was incredible community excitement, interest, and input on this issue — lots of very good ideas," says Bonnie Biemer, administrator of the city's Office of Health and Environment. "The Brownfields Working Group, which evolved from the Environmental Practitioner's Group in September 1994, continues to report to the EC Executive Committee to keep these communication channels open." Two members of the EC Executive Committee serve on the Brownfields Working Group.

Meeting the Challenge

In 1995, Louisville's brownfields program was given a major boost when EPA awarded the city a $200,000 Brownfield Pilot Site grant. With this money, officials planned to launch site assessment activities in targeted EC areas, including Louisville's West End, the location of the Ni-Chro Plating facility. Because Louisville Dryer had expressed interest in buying the neighboring Ni-Chro plant — a move that would provide jobs and tax revenues for the local community — city officials believed this site would make a good "pilot project" to kick off their brownfields program. "The idea was that through our activities at this site, we would develop a process that could be transferred and used at other sites," says Rich Campbell.

A major barrier at Ni-Chro Plating's site was the fact that almost $200,000 of liens saddled the property, while its appraised value was only one-sixth this amount, roughly $35,000. Because of this discrepancy, the site never would move forward unless this burden were lifted. In July 1995, the mayor of Louisville called EPA Region 4, requesting that the lien on the property be released. He stressed his desire to make the property a demonstration site under EPA's Brownfields Pilot Site grant. When agency personnel looked into the matter, they determined that, in fact, the seven-year statute of limitations had expired on the property, and the lien was forgiven. Weeks later, the property was auctioned off at the courthouse door.

The Landbank Authority, a real estate holding company that manages tax-foreclosed properties in Louisville, bid $22,000 for the property — the amount the city was owed in costs, liens, and back taxes. A city official describes the Landbank as "a machine that turns derelict and abandoned, tax-delinquent land in the inner city into clean, vacant lots with clear titles for sale and ready for development." In the past eight years, the authority has returned to productive use more than 1,000 parcels, roughly 25 percent of the vacant structures in Louisville.

Once the Landbank Authority held title to the former Ni-Chro Plating site in fall 1995, the city began conducting additional assessment and sampling activities. City officials understood that Louisville Dryer needed to have a strong comfort level about the site and, as such, kept the company appraised of all environmental work, even though formal sale negotiations would not begin for another a year. "Our main concern was that the property used to be a metal plating company, and we knew there were a lot of hazardous chemicals," says Phil Guthrie, general manager of the Louisville Dryer Co. "First, we wanted to make sure everything was removed; second, we wanted a soil analysis done; third, we wanted to look at the structural integrity of the building. We wanted to have a really good feeling about the land and the facility itself."

Environmental assessments revealed only nominal contamination at the site. "We didn't find much of a problem," says the city's Bonnie Biemer. "Perception is much worse than reality in most of these brownfield situations." In one area behind the building, however, surface soil was found to contain 1,500 parts per million (ppm) of lead. In its proposed Site Management Plan, submitted to the Kentucky Department of Environmental Protection (DEP) in June 1996, the city proposed removing this hotspot and disposing the soils off-site. Samples taken at other areas around the property did not exceed state levels of concern for human health and, therefore, the city proposed leaving these soils on-site, with gravel and the existing building serving as a cap.

Three community meetings were held between the Brownfields Working Group and neighborhood residents. Officials learned that while residents near Louisville Dryer were angry about some existing problems including dust, truck traffic, on-street parking, and the eyesore of outdoor equipment storage, they were only mildly concerned about environmental remediation at the site. According to the city's Biemer, Louisville Dryer "acted like a good neighbor" and implemented measures to lessen the company's impact on neighboring residents (e.g., they developed a new entranceway to minimize traffic and placed a fence that concealed the industrial yard from the neighborhood). "One of my primary goals was to build positive relations with the neighborhood," says Louisville Dryer's general manager, Phil Guthrie. The working group also coordinated a meeting with city traffic engineers in order to address the traffic and parking problems.

Site work was proceeding in 1996 when another question emerged: How could proceeds from the sale of the Ni-Chro property, and other future brownfields sites, be retained for use in the Louisville brownfields program? "Normally proceeds would go back to the Landbank Authority, which would then dispose the funds to the four taxing entities owed the money — i.e., the state, county, city, or school district — but in this case we wanted the money to be retained for acquisition and remediation of future brownfield sites," says EPA's Rich Campbell. Other than EPA's $200,000 brownfield grant, the Office of Health and Environment had almost no public money dedicated to brownfield site characterization and cleanup activities. Therefore, city officials were intent on keeping proceeds from the Ni-Chro Plating facility sale for future brownfields work. Members of the Louisville Landbank (representing the different taxing entities) apparently support the idea, but the Landbank's by-laws need to be amended to allow such a change. Discussing these issues and drafting appropriate amendments has taken several months.

In the summer of 1996, new managers at Louisville Dryer conducted their own inspection of Ni-Chro Plating's buildings and determined that widespread structural problems existed. In fact, company officials argued, the property's correct value is closer to zero than the assessed value of $35,000. So, once again, Louisville Dryer and the city are back at the table negotiating price. But there is another complication. The state has not yet approved the Site Management Plan submitted by the city in June 1996. Until that plan is approved and a No Further Remediation letter is issued, Louisville Dryer officials say that they will not proceed. (The No Further Remediation letter would become effective upon approval of the Site Management Plan; however, if the plan were not fully complied with, the letter would become void.)

In fact, the state is delaying approval of the Site Management Plan — not because of issues connected to the former Ni-Chro Plating site, but because of uncertain site conditions on the immediately adjacent rail yard property. State officials are concerned about possible off-site contamination from the Norfolk-Southern rail facility and have requested that a deed restriction (or some other effective institutional control) be put in place to ensure that the property is confined to industrial use. Norfolk-Southern is considering the request but does not have to accept the deed restriction. City officials note, with a hint of frustration, that soil removal and sale negotiations at the Ni-Chro Plating site remain on hold until this matter is settled.

Regulatory Framework

In its 1996 legislative session, the State of Kentucky passed brownfields legislation that offers No Further Remediation Letters to public entities for sites where a remediation plan has been successfully completed. "Public entities" include the State of Kentucky, a county, city, urban-county government, charter county government, or corporations set up on behalf of local government.

In this case, the City of Louisville submitted a proposed Site Management Plan, along with a request for a No Further Remediation Letter, to DEP officials in June 1996. The state has not yet approved the plan.

Financing

Louisville's brownfield program has received strong federal assistance in recent years. First, the city was awarded a $200,000 EPA Brownfields Pilot Site grant in 1995. In addition, EPA provided the program a $75,000 "seed grant" through the state. The city also secured $6.5 million in preliminary private and foundation commitments to purchase stock in a new Community Development Bank, an institution that will: 1) provide credit and stimulate business/housing opportunities in select areas; and 2) provide loans to emerging businesses that employ low and moderate-income residents. The remaining funds will be used to craft customized job training for residents in the Enterprise Community area. These moneys — while not specifically earmarked for brownfield projects — provide an investor-friendly climate that encourages cleanup and redevelopment of older, industrial properties within these economically depressed areas.

In 1995, Louisville received a total of $7 million from HUD in support of its Enterprise Community (EC) plans, a portion of which will be used to fund brownfield activities. This money primarily will be used to back the city's new Community Development Bank.

Cleanup (soil removal) at the Ni-Chro Plating property has not taken place yet, as city officials are waiting for the state to approve the Site Management Plan. Officials anticipate paying for remediation with proceeds from the property sale.

Impacts

In the fall of 1996, the city allowed Louisville Dryer Co. to move into a portion of the Ni-Chro Plating building (despite the fact that site remediation was pending) in order to accommodate the company's expansion needs. Louisville Dryer already has brought on 15 additional workers, for a total of 40 employees. "We're here to stay, with the opportunity to grow," says Louisville Dryer's general manager, Phil Guthrie.

Lessons Learned

According to participants involved with this project, redevelopment of the Ni-Chro Plating site was facilitated by the following:

Strong Public Sector Involvement

This project has been complicated by an array of factors, including environmental contamination at the site and uncertain remediation requirements. What seems clear is that without involvement by the City of Louisville, this deal likely would have gone nowhere. The city served a critical role as "brownfield broker," overseeing relations between the Kentucky DEP, the Landbank Authority, and the prospective purchaser, Louisville Dryer Company. City officials arranged for the lien to be released by EPA, conducted site assessments, and drafted the Site Management Plan for submittal to DEP. In addition, the city dedicated funds to this project (for personnel and site assessment) from grant money provided under EPA's Brownfields Pilot Site Program. Because of the city's involvement, Louisville Dryer has been able to remain involved in a real estate transaction that it might otherwise have abandoned long ago.

Effective Community Outreach

Officials from the Louisville Dryer Company (and its predecessor Clemco) worked closely with the surrounding neighborhood, with assistance from the city's Brownfields Working Group. "When you have old communities where industry and homes are mixed together, you have to have a structure of communication between the businesses and the residents," says the city's Biemer. "If you don't have community buy-in from the start, it could cause big problems later on."

The Brownfields Working Group

When Louisville officials launched their brownfields program, the first priority was formation of a Brownfields Working Group. "The job of the Brownfields Working Group is to create a new process for redevelopment that will break down the usual brownfield barriers (liability issues, prohibitive costs, and long drawn-out time frames) and provide an easier, more user-friendly system," says the city's Biemer. "It's a sort of 'think tank' for planning and policy development. But we saw that we needed an entity to actually obtain land — a mechanism for holding and turning over property. In the case of the pilot, that entity is the Landbank Authority."

Biemer adds, however, that the Landbank Authority has addressed only tax-foreclosable property, a subset of the total brownfields picture in Louisville. The city still needs to identify a process for acquiring and proactively marketing brownfield sites that are not tax-delinquent.

"No centralized decision-making body exists to oversee brownfield issues," Biemer explains. "That's what we're struggling with right now. We want the brownfield program to have a home — to be institutionalized. But in light of diminishing government resources, we are trying to use existing resources as much as possible and not create whole new bureaucracies." Biemer speculates that the city's Office of Economic Development will likely be the new home for Louisville's brownfield program, with the Office of Health and Environment serving in a technical advisory position and administering the city's Brownfields Data Base.

Contacts

Rich Campbell
EPA Region 4
(on a two-year assignment to the City of Louisville)
(502) 574-2511

Bonnie Biemer
Administrator
City of Louisville's Office of Health and Environment
(502) 574-3271

Other Brownfield Publications from the Northeast-Midwest Institute

Coming Clean for Economic Development: A Resource Book on Environmental Cleanup and Economic Development Opportunities **Revised & Updated**
By Charles Bartsch and Elizabeth Collaton
Environmental concerns, traditionally viewed as peripheral by economic development practitioners, now play an important role in the economic revitalization process. Issues such as environmental cleanup and reuse of contaminated industrial sites occupy a prominent place in the sustainability discussion. This resource guidebook, targeted to local economic development practitioners, identifies cross-cutting economic development and environmental cleanup opportunities and common environmental rules. It provides these practitioners with information on state voluntary cleanup programs in 49 states and resources needed to make informed decisions when dealing with a variety of environmental considerations. *177 pages. $36.*

Industrial Site Reuse, Contamination, and Urban Redevelopment: Coping With the Challenges of Brownfields
By Charles Bartsch and Elizabeth Collaton
Despite the many benefits of site reuse — such as restoration of centrally-located economic centers, more efficient use of infrastructure systems, and increased local tax revenues and jobs — several factors undermine the desirability of such properties. In addition to analyzing the legal, economic, and environmental challenges associated with "brownfields," this report highlights case studies of successful partnerships that cleaned up polluted sites. *49 pages. $18.*

New Life for Old Buildings: Confronting the Environmental and Economic Issues to Industrial Reuse
By Charles Bartsch, Carol Andress, Deborah Cooney and Jocelyn Seitzman
Mills, factories, and machine shops lie abandoned by the thousands nationwide. Many obstacles deter their return to productive use. ***New Life*** examines the scope of the environmental problems plaguing industrial redevelopment and their effects on project finance. The book analyzes federal and state liability laws and the uncertainties over what constitutes a clean site. *105 pages. $18. Case studies.*

Revival of Contaminated Industrial Sites: Case Studies
By Charles Bartsch, Carol Andress, Deborah Cooney and Jocelyn Seitzman
This report focuses on the case studies of the 15 communities referred to in ***New Life for Old Buildings***. It shows how communities have worked with developers and lenders, packaged incentives, and formed public-private partnerships to successfully revive and reuse contaminated industrial sites. *44 pages. $12. Case studies.*